Beyond Romance

Beyond Romance
Making Love Last

by
Robert H. Simmons, Ph.D.

New Horizon Press
Far Hills, New Jersey

New Horizon Press
P.O. Box 669
Far Hills, NJ 07931

Simmons, Robert H.:
Beyond Romance: Making Love Last

Cover Design: Robert Aulicino
Interior Design: Susan M. Sanderson
Library of Congress Control Number: 2004108084
ISBN: 0-88282-255-1
New Horizon Press
Manufactured in Canada

2009   2008   2007   2006   2005 / 5   4   3   2   1

Dedication
to
Mia Mitchell Simmons

Ver ad finim

My deepest appreciation to my wife, Mia Mitchell Simmons, whose profound, devoted love and support enable me to strive for and sometimes reach my highest creative potential. The rhythm and harmony which flow between us are a significant part of our lives. Whether we are engaged in our shared life's work or in working out our struggles; sharing our fears and sadness or our manifold joys, she is devoted to nurturing those aspects that are essential ingredients in the quality of our lives together.

She is, as the ancient motto of the Clan Mitchell states—

True to the end.

Human love is so obscured by the inflations and commotions of romance that we almost never look for love in its own right, and we hardly know what to look for when we do search. But as we learn love's characteristics and attitudes, we can begin to see love within us revealed in our feelings, in the spontaneous flow of warmth that surges toward another person, in small unnoticed acts of relatedness that make up the secret fabric of our daily lives.

Robert A. Johnson

Contents

Author's Note

This book is based on extensive personal interviews with men and women in relationships, experience counseling couples and a thorough study of the available literature. Fictitious identities and names have been given to characters in this book in order to protect privacy. Some characters may be composites. For the purposes of simplifying usage, the pronouns *his* and *her* are sometimes used interchangeably.

Acknowledgments

In the journey that brought me to the inevitable writing of this book, I have many to thank. Foremost are my parents, Chester Spaulding Simmons and Karolyn Van Ness Simmons, who were steadfast in their devotion to each other and to their children. They lived right inside their intentional love and, in so doing, they also imparted big lessons in "stick-to-it-iveness" and staying "through thick and thin"—which was their language for commitment.

From my daughter Karolyn and son-in-law Rick Wilson I learned that the glue of a marriage is commitment and loyalty. I am grateful to each of my other children—Rachael, for teaching me the joy and importance of being true to yourself; Richard and his wife Shulan, who allowed me to experience the developmental stages of their relationship; Drew and his partner, Monica Leon Garrido, who have found a path of peace together. For their trust and openness with me, I am so very thankful. And an appreciation goes to my brother Van Ness Howard and his wonderful wife Dorothy Mae Biasi Simmons, whose long-lasting love is a loadstar of devoted, mature, intentional love lived every day. I am grateful to them for their continuing example. My twin brother Dick and his wife Carol have always represented commitment and loyalty through the years. My thanks also go to my brother-in-law George Douglas Mitchell and his wife Claire, who are heroic partners in their marriage; they are a model of devotion.

Colleagues at California State University Los Angeles, Professors Eugene Dvorin, Benjamin Smith, Ted Anagnoson, Stephen Ma, John Hauk, Tom Rusch, Harry Brand, Dean Donald Dewey and many others provided important professional support along the way. My Australian colleagues, Professors Roger Wettenhall, Bruce Davis, Mike Wood and Ralph Chapman, great friends and great hosts, made me welcome and contributed to me professionally in important areas.

To Nina Negranti, Esq., a heartfelt thank you for her continuing support through the years and for her constant encouragement. She never lost faith in this effort and for that I am forever grateful. Sincere thanks to Jeffrey R. Stein, Esq. and his wife Pamela Burton Stein, Marriage and Family Counselor and Ph.D. candidate, who have lived the chapters of this book, for their long-lasting friendship, continuous support and faith in this effort. To Robert and Linda Takken and Tom and Donna Dalton, a sincere thank you for their continuous friendship and support. To Steve Caminiti and his wife Carole Kaufman, whose heartfelt support of my efforts helped breathe life into this book, I am grateful. To Danny Lickness, M.D. and Michael deWitt Clayton, M.D., I give my thanks for their steadfast encouragement.

Joan Borysenko, Ph.D., Michael F. Myers, M.D., Roy W. Menninger, M.D., Stanley Gene Sateren, M.D., Linda Stoer-Scaggs, Ph.D., John Birsner, Jr., M.D. , Dugald D. Chisholm, M.D., Randolph J. Gould, M.D., Judy Fried Siegel, M.D., Pamela Stones, Ph.D., Mamta Gautam, M.D., Mano Murty, M.D., and William Zeckhausen, D. Min. provided inspiration through their books and through their friendships. I met them all through the PhysicianWellness Conference I directed. They each are profoundly committed to the psychological and spiritual health of marriages. To Marie Cowan, who has worked through the pages of this book and made cogent and valuable suggestions, I am deeply thankful. To Dinah Hatton, my friend of many years who read the manuscript thoroughly and made significant suggestions that enhanced my efforts, I express my deep gratitude. Kate Perry Harding and Lauren Oliver, Ph.D. were there in the beginning and helped to cultivate the fertile soil that gave root to the ideas found in this book. To Kathleen Atkinson, Ph.D., my professional colleague who has made significant contributions to my work through the years, many thanks for her continuing encouragement. My thanks to Claude Steiner, Ph.D., whose vision and writing provided inspiration to this work. And thanks to Vicki Carter Hotaling, Susan King, MFCC, Cliff Branch, Betty Branch, MFCC, Mele-Phyllis Mar, Lisa Lester, Terri Trew, M.S.W., L.C.S.W., Mark Welch, teacher and song-writer, and the many others who lent their encouragement and support to my work.

To my wife, Mia Mitchell Simmons—ever-present with her encouragement, skillful attention to detail and devoted love—I am profoundly indebted and forever grateful. Hers has been a valued and vital contribution.

To my publisher Dr. Joan S. Dunphy, New Horizon Press, I express my deepest gratitude for her faith in the distinctive message in this book and for her key suggestions which considerably improved the book. Lynda Hatch, consummate editor, was essential to every phase of this effort. Many kudos and many thanks for her reassurances. She never failed to deliver the support, information and guidance I required to keep my mind steady and my eye on the task. My thanks to Catherine Finegan, production editor, whose impeccable editing added significantly to this book. Her gracious manner was a special delight to the process of bringing this book to fruition. I am grateful for the full and complete dedication of the entire team at New Horizon Press. They embraced this project with enthusiasm and sustained their efforts through to publication.

Finally, I acknowledge the indispensably creative talents of Susan Stewart, my personal editor, who helped to bring significant comprehension to the disparate materials I have been gathering over twenty-five years. Her guidance, skill and creativity gave shape and coherence to the concepts, insights and lessons offered here.

Prologue

And life is what we make it, always has been, always will be.
Anna Mary Robertson, AKA
Grandma Moses

At a time when the *disposable* marriage has reached an all-time high (the divorce rate has tripled since the 1960s), many, many couples earnestly search for ways to avoid ending their marriages. More and more couples are exploring new alternatives for transforming unrewarding and unsatisfying relationships into fulfilling, intimate and lifelong partnerships. I believe society is witnessing the emergence of a surprising modern trend: In my experience couples are working harder than ever before to stay together.

When two people choose each other, a great opportunity is provided for a lifelong merging and integration of two individuals. In this act, they each *commit* to creating a connection, a mutual devotion and a combination of energy that hopefully will offer great fulfillment and reward. When two people are attuned to each other, their movements, feelings and thoughts can diminish, and perhaps even eliminate, friction and separatism. Yet this cannot be achieved without difficult, dedicated work—both by the partners together and by each one individually. The hostile dance that characterizes much of the rancor between partners can only be stopped by working through the difficulties. When the individuals are willing and the work is undertaken and continued, each partner will feel connected, empowered and capable of creating a mature and lasting love.

This book is designed to help committed partners *intentionally* develop their relationships. One of the goals is to help partners who are thoroughly committed to each other become fully empowered companions who, separately and together, can manage their anger, fear, joy and sadness in powerful, healing and rewarding ways. The exercises, guidelines and information in this book are designed to help partners use the struggle between themselves to develop insight, understanding and skills that will enhance their communication, enrich their intimacy and amplify their support for each other. Couples reading this book will come to understand that a relationship is a developmental journey—a journey they can take either consciously or unconsciously. The unconscious journey leads to disaster. The conscious one is challenging and exciting and leads to a mutually rewarding future.

Romance is a heady illusion that promises much, but when the inevitable disappointments set in after the honeymoon, reality often dissipates early passion of attraction. The fire of romance dies, the ashes turn cold and hearts turn to stone. The disappointments may be sad, bitter, angering and often bewildering, giving rise to wondering *why, how?* This book will focus on what happens when the illusion of romance crumbles and everyday routines and obligations take hold. The message centers upon the importance of intentional love in the achievement of a deep, meaningful and rewarding relationship. This intentional love then becomes the foundation for a profound and lasting love, sustained by commitment and rewarded by devotion, passion and joy.

Couples in long-term marriages who put conscious effort into the development of their marriages, my and other research and experience shows, become happier as their marriages age; the partners become more affectionate, more communicative, more considerate and more forgiving. Young love, romantic love, is like a flame—captivating, passionate and fierce; but it may also be hypnotic, ephemeral and delusional. It burns fast and bright and dies swiftly. The love of the committed heart is devoted, deep-burning, unquenchable. If it is to last, romantic love must be transformed into a profound, authentic and rewarding love—intentional love. When achieved, intentional love is devoted and mature—the true love of our hearts' desire.

To achieve this end, committed partners need to intentionally create the relationship they seek within their own marriage. When conflicts occur they must recognize and embrace them as opportunities for growth and change rather than discouraging moments of stress and disappointment. This book will teach couples how they may effectively transform controversy into mutual devotion and empowerment. If you and your partner embark upon it, the ultimate destination of your journey is mature love, an embodiment of commitment, friendship, compatibility, affection and sensuality. That journey begins with the acceptance that love is an intentional choice you make every day.

Using This Book
to Make Love Last

Good marriages seem effortless to those on the outside
but a lot of good care goes into them...
                                                    Merle Shain

This book may be used in the following four ways: 1) by couples seeking to increase their self-awareness and enrich their relationship independently of a therapist or counselor; 2) by participants in Couples Enrichment Workshops or other therapeutic couples groups; 3) by couples who are engaged in ongoing counseling or therapy or 4) by singles who wish to improve their self-awareness in preparation for successful coupled relationships. This book can enhance and propel the work for all those who seek to create and sustain a rewarding, abiding and loving relationship.

Each chapter in the three sections of the book builds upon the concepts taught in the previous pages. It is recommended that you tackle them in sequence. Then do the one or more exercises called *Endeavors*.

You may read through the whole book first, omitting the Endeavors, and then begin again with chapter 1 and complete Endeavors as you go, or simply begin the work with chapter 1.

Singles using this book are encouraged to complete the exercises, as are partners working separately. While some elements of certain exercises are structured for partners, singles can and should complete the questions and reflections. In this way singles will better know themselves and prepare for becoming part of successful partnerships.

Each partner should complete, independently of the other, the questions and tasks of the Endeavors. Copy the Endeavors for the second partner. If it's inconvenient to make copies, each partner may wish to purchase a book. Having your own copy of the book will allow you to underline, highlight or make notes in the margins without invading or influencing the other's. Each partner should also have a notepad, notebook or journal in which to write responses.

Don't rush through the Endeavors; some will be easier and take less time to complete than others. Finish each one as thoroughly and honestly as possible. Remember, to make your marriage a thriving one takes committed work; the tasks you complete using the guided Endeavors will help you make that happen. Each Endeavor contains mutual activities focused on accomplishing: 1) greater understanding of yourself; 2) greater understanding of your partner and 3) greater understanding of the partnership and relationship you want to attain. They will help you identify those areas in your relationship that work well and deserve to be celebrated and those where greater awareness and more work is needed.

Complete the Endeavors in the order in which they appear. They are designed to build, one upon the other, to deepen your relationship. Each one begins with an Overview, followed by Activities. The Endeavor is not complete until you Share the Process, which will illuminate each partner's feelings and clear up confusions. Each one ends with a specific expression of Appreciation and a confirmation of your love.

Guidelines for Creating Emotionally Safe Conversations

Because some of the activities involve tapping uncomfortable or painful feelings, it will be important to feel emotionally safe enough to express them. Think about the ways in which you sometimes feel threatened, frightened or emotionally at risk when you are engaged in conversations with your partner. Then compose a list of the conditions to which you will both agree when doing the activities in this book. To help you get started, here is a preliminary list of guidelines.

1. Look directly into each other's eyes and listen without interruption.
2. Give each other all the time needed to share feelings fully and honestly.
3. Do not defend or explain yourselves—simply *listen, listen, listen.*
4. Do not attack or blame each other.
5. Listen through the words being said to hear the feelings expressed.
6. Be empathic, compassionate, considerate and kind.
7. Do not judge each other.
8. Do not dominate the conversation or talk over each other.
9. "Check in" with each other, when needed, to see whether or not you have understood what was said.

Now add three more of your own conditions, write them down, make a copy of this list, title it *Guidelines for Safe Communication* and abide by it. Keep this list handy during your discussions as a gentle reminder of your agreement to stay within the emotionally safe territory that makes this work productive.

It is helpful, if not crucial, to make a commitment to each other out loud, holding hands and looking into each other's eyes:

I commit to complete this book and its Endeavors with you, no matter how difficult it may seem.

Long, successful experience with a great number of couples leads me to reassure you that if you do the work that is suggested here, your marriage will emerge enhanced, whole, stronger and more rewarding. Persevere and the rewards will be great.

Beyond Romance

PART I:
THE ARDUOUS JOURNEY

Chapter 1

The Illusion of Romantic Love

*Romance has been elegantly defined
as the offspring of fiction and love.*
Benjamin Disraeli

Why is it that the first sparks of romance promise so much and turn so quickly to ashes? Because that first fiery encounter is an illusion! The glow of romance is that breathtaking enticement which lures people into seeking a mate. It provides extraordinary intensity, drama, sensory stimulation, excitement, fireworks, a high. We chase the illusory promise of romance, because it is so heady, so appealing.

A shameless tease, romance promises much, but delivers little. Maintenance of romance is costly, requiring increasing amounts of emotional energy to retain the same euphoria. Guided by recklessness, romantic love takes its subjects for an exciting roller coaster ride. Romance burns bright, fast, hot—then it's gone. And when romance and reality collide, as they eventually do, one of these opposite forces will come out the winner, one the loser. If the need for romance prevails, the relationship ends and one or both partners continue the forlorn search for the eternal romantic encounter. If reality wins, a couple successfully maneuvers the first and necessary phase of their lasting relationship.

Anne Morrow Lindbergh, in *Gifts from the Sea*, compares this first phase of a relationship to the double sunrise shell: "Two flawless halves bound together with a single hinge, meeting each other at every point, the dawn of a new day spreading on each face. It is a world to itself." Morrow points out that this beautiful, fragile state of being is fleeting and must give way to growth and submit to change in the cycle of life. There is no holding of a relationship to a single form. While this original essence of a relationship is never lost, it becomes immersed in the realities of life.

Merle Shain observed in *Courage My Love*, "It's odd that the highly perishable commodity, passionate love, with its limited shelf life, is thought to be a suitable foundation on which to hang the whole exhaustive structure of family and property and tradition, but we rarely question it."

In our eagerness to build a lifetime marriage on the transitory foundation of romance we soon find out that our ideal is flimsy, unreliable building material for the stable foundation needed to support a lasting, healthy relationship.

Some people seek a phantom sometimes known as a *soulmate*. In the throes of passionate romance, they feel that they have found their soulmates. The illusion of the soulmate is a childlike hope that a partner will be exactly as a person expects.

Unfortunately, these hidden hopes and expectations are soon dashed as reality sets in. The truth is that we want our partners to be the perfect parents we never had and to parent us with the unconditional love we deeply seek. When the partner a person has labeled a soulmate disappoints, when he or she turns out to be unable or unwilling to fulfill the fantasy and give the person what he or she seeks, disillusionment results and the couple finds their relationship in trouble without knowing why.

Peter and Rebecca, one couple I counseled, met in their twenties as workmates. They were attracted to each other and acknowledged a mutual crush but did nothing about it. Twenty years later, they met again and fell head over heels in love. On the surface, it was a heavenly match. Intelligent, well-educated, mature and stable, they found in each other a mutual sensuality and excitement that had been missing in previous relationships. They were open and honest with each other and delighted in spending hours together walking, hiking, talking and making love. It was, they both thought, the romance they'd always been seeking. They each began to think about marriage. However, eight months later, Peter announced he wanted to break the relationship up, stunning Rebecca and wounding them both. When she begged him to tell her why, Peter could only speak in vague generalities, saying things like "You're not the woman I thought you were," "You don't really listen to me," and "We're just too different."

The mistake each partner made was the belief that the other would completely fulfill the image he or she wanted him or her to be. Their expectations were unrealistic. Peter fell in love with a vision of what he wanted Rebecca to be. When she fell short of that, Peter decided—without sharing his feelings with Rebecca first—to end the relationship. His hidden hopes for a paragon, an always kind, attentive, conservative, easy-going woman, were dashed when the reality of Rebecca's humanness set in. He knew the relationship was in trouble, but he didn't know why, so he decided he had to end it. As we'll see later, Peter and Rebecca eventually reunited only to break up again—and again. Ultimately, they were not able to use the value of the romantic stage that began their relationship as a bridge to greater understanding.

In fact, romance can be a healthy catalyst, a bridge into the challenge of marriage. However, romance is transitory; alone it cannot sustain a relationship. Here is what Sam Keen, in *Fire in the Belly*, says about romance:

If you consider marriage a lifelong romance, you are certain to be disillusioned. The shallowest of complaints is that marriage destroys romance. Of course it does. Marriage is designed to allow two people to fall out of love and into reality.

True love is built on intimacy. Intimacy's real passion is only achieved by combining the five necessary elements for a mature relationship: friendship, compatibility, affection, commitment and sensuality. The key to true passion is not illusory romance, but intimacy. One of the goals of what we will call *intentional love* is to achieve this intimacy which, in turn, will ignite the passion sought and lost in the first stage of relationships—the romantic stage. When you and your partner accept that romance is only the beginning, you can achieve profound intimacy—true love's reward.

A good and rewarding marriage can only be created with *conscious awareness* on the part of both partners. Two people who choose each other have the power and the ability to develop their relationship if they do so consciously and purposefully. When troubled, a committed relationship cannot be repaired by hope alone, nor will neglect, denial or avoidance gain the end each partner desires. It is the energy and commitment of the partners and a willingness to work on their relationship that will make a marriage sound and joyful.

It is important to understand that marriages move through stages and it's vital that both partners understand and undertake the elements of their journey together. Such a commitment requires the development of both partners' understanding of themselves and the other partner.

A successful marriage is one wherein the partners have learned to manage their strong feelings in a constructive manner, one that is satisfying, rewarding and sustaining, even amidst sorrow, tragedy and adversity.

There are five distinct developmental stages in marriage, each with its own set of definable characteristics, which we will explore in later chapters. The reason relationships experience trouble is that most couples traverse these stages blindly. In this book we will see how couples who attend these stages with thoughtful determination can create remarkable harmony. The creation of such harmony is an intentional choice. Couples who are unaware or unwilling to work through these stages can get stuck, forever frozen in an unhappy, disillusioned state.

Let me repeat, the keys to developing a conscious marriage are intention, choice and the willingness to become *emotionally literate*. Before people had words to convey them, our emotions were the very first language we used. As we developed words to describe them, we lost the ability to see clearly the connection between our emotions and how we behave. Emotions still drive our behavior, but because of the veil of language we are blinded and do not see or understand our feelings clearly. Thus whenever our emotionally-driven behavior is challenged, as it may be in a partnership in which we do not see our needs met, we blame, defend or attack.

Partners must strive to look within and find emotional literacy, which means being alert to fears and angers; joys and sadness; grief, guilt, envy and shame, including how they are contained within and how they are expressed. It means developing a highly conscious knowledge of the link between the emotional life and behavior. Without this consciousness, people are emotionally illiterate, enslaved by our own unconscious, knee-jerk reactions to emotions.

I can't promise that it will be easy for each partner traveling the road to emotional literacy. It may be rough and painful. But the rewards are a fuller, richer, happier life filled with a warm, honest and loving relationship. You must start with sincere intention and with some basic truths.

First, let us look at ten *Romantic Illusions* that undergird the false beliefs many people have about selecting a partner and create the setup for illusory thinking about marriage. These often lead to disappointment, disillusionment, discontentment and loss. Paired with the *Marital Realities* that characterize the underpinnings of a healthy marriage, these self-delusions must be understood by each partner in order to develop a conscious, emotionally literate and successful marriage.

Table 1

Romantic Illusions and Marital Realities

Romantic Illusion #1 Belief in the magic of enchantment— love will fuse us into soulmates and make us feel whole and complete.	**Marital Reality #1** Marriage provides an opportunity for fulfillment and wholeness, but partners must actively work together to obtain them.
Romantic Illusion #2 Belief that if we truly love each other, romance will always flourish.	**Marital Reality #2** Marriage requires awareness that feelings of love wax and wane.
Romantic Illusion #3 Belief that our mates will change for us if they truly love us.	**Marital Reality #3** We must accept our mates as they are and know that working on a marriage is integral to its health.
Romantic Illusion #4 Belief in the fantasy of the all-knowing partner, that our mate should understand us and know how we feel, what we need and what we are thinking at all times.	**Marital Reality #4** No one can fully know another— both partners need to develop understanding rooted in acceptance and knowledge.
Romantic Illusion #5 Belief that in marriage passion and intensity must be constant and unchanging.	**Marital Reality #5** Marriages evolve through growth, disintegration, rebirth and reintegration. This keeps the marriage vital and alive.

Romantic Illusion #6 Belief that continuous togetherness is essential to love.	**Marital Reality #6** Partners need time for their own privacy, solitude, diversion and reflection.
Romantic Illusion #7 Belief that if conflict exists in marriage, then love has taken flight.	**Marital Reality #7** Conflict is to be expected and offers opportunities for the marriage to grow when managed constructively.
Romantic Illusion #8 Belief that sexual interest is a constant of love and romance.	**Marital Reality #8** Sexual interest is variable, rarely understood or openly talked about. Differences must be honored and respected. Where sexual disinterest occurs, help is necessary to resolve the problem.
Romantic Illusion #9 Belief that if we are feeling personally unfulfilled in the marriage, our partner must be at fault.	**Marital Reality #9** We are responsible for our own feelings. Attacking and blaming a partner and defending ourselves are efforts to shift the blame.
Romantic Illusion #10 Belief that a good marriage will always be fair and equal.	**Marital Reality #10** The trap of fairness is transcended by giving and receiving without keeping track. When we love without expectations, do not measure what is returned, receive what is given and give without qualms, then real partnership and friendship can flourish.

Following this chapter are the first two Endeavors. In the first Endeavor, "Our Relationship—Illusions and Realities," you will each discover the ideas—true or false—you hold about your relationship and about marriage in general. In the Endeavor "Do You See What I See?" you will uncover some remarkable discrepancies between what's real and what you *perceive* is real. Complete both Endeavors before moving on to chapter 2. Your answers will form a solid foundation for the challenges ahead.

The next two chapters deal with two important concepts that must be understood before we can begin to find our way back to the ideal of love. They are the concepts of *developmental stages* (both as individuals and as a couple) and the *inner family theater.*

As we begin to work together and clear away the illusion of romance, the chaos of disillusionment often takes its place. This may be a frightening place to be. But it is only a temporary phase. Let me reassure you, if you are willing to travel the road, the journey will provide a greater understanding of yourself, your partner and your marriage. You and your partner will achieve a far greater love—*beyond romance.*

Endeavor: Our Relationship—Illusions and Realities

Overview

This first Endeavor will help you enrich your marriage through greater understanding of yourself, your beliefs and your expectations. The guided dialogue is designed to reveal, in an emotionally safe way, the unconscious, undisclosed assumptions you've made. These unspoken ideas, beliefs and expectations may be impeding the healthy development of your relationship. Once revealed and identified, they can be understood. Then steps can be taken to remove these blocks so you can move forward in your life together with your partner.

Activities

Take some time apart to respond to the statements and questions that follow. Write your answers in your separate notebooks.

1. **Exploring Romantic Illusions and Marital Realities**
    a. Review the Romantic Illusions listed earlier in this chapter and select the ones that you brought to your relationship. Write explanations of the ones you selected in your notebook.
    b. Review the listing of Marital Realities and identify which ones you recognize in your marriage now. Write these in your notebook and explain how these realizations have come about.
    c. Briefly explore whether your beliefs and expectations about your partnership have been met.

2. **How Do I Feel about My Marriage Now?**
    Explore your feelings about the current state of your relationship with your partner. Answer the following questions.
    a. Have there been disappointments? Explain what they are.
    b. What bothers you about conflicts with your partner?
    c. Do you think your love can change your partner?
    d. Is there something your partner finds annoying about you that you wish he or she would just accept?

e. When you are feeling down or disgruntled, is it usually because of something your partner has done or not done?

f. Do you ever find yourself wondering why your partner hasn't done anything nice for you lately?

g. What are some things you would like your partner to do for you?

h. Do you wonder whether your partner noticed the last two or three things you did for him or her? How do you feel about his or her taking you for granted?

i. Do you worry that if you're not always together, your relationship is in jeopardy?

j. How often have you found yourself wishing your partner could just intuit what you need?

k. Do you believe that you know your partner so well that you can read what he or she thinks, feels or desires?

Sit down together and, in an unhurried way, take turns reading your responses to your partner. Listen carefully, empathically and without interrupting. Remember to use the Guidelines for Safe Communication.

Sharing the Process

Uncensored thoughts are usually the most truthful, so don't agonize over your answers to this exercise. Your replies should be shared verbally, not written out.

Teasing, joking and sarcasm are basically cruel and defeat intimacy; such retorts mock the other partner and distance the person using such measures from a loving connection with his or her partner. They have no place in these activities and dialogues.

Now respond to the following questions together.

• What is the most significant thing you learned about yourself?
• What is the most significant thing you learned about your partner?
• What is the most difficult aspect of sharing your responses?
• What is the most satisfying aspect?

Appreciations
- Share one thing you appreciate about your partner. Be focused and specific. For example, "I really appreciated your honesty when you identified your unmet expectations about our relationship."

Close With—
- Close each Endeavor with a warm hug and a genuine "I love you." Such expression of affection may not always come naturally, especially when the material you've each worked on has brought up difficult or painful issues. However, even if you are not feeling particularly loving at the moment, you are encouraged to express your love for each other anyway. For it is your underlying love, after all, that is fueling this work and will make it succeed in bringing you closer even though you have brought to the surface differing points of view and conflicts.

Endeavor: Do You See What I See?

Overview

In every long lasting relationship, as time passes, the things one partner thinks he or she knows about a partner distort, creating a haze of disappointments, failed expectations and faded hopes. This Endeavor is focused on rediscovering yourself and your partner in a very different way—deepening your understanding and creating the prelude to further work. Before you proceed, please review the Guidelines for Safe Communication. Add to them if you need to, fine tune them and recommit to using them.

During the sharing part of this Endeavor, as I've said before, be sure to speak each other's name and look into each other's eyes. Too often we take our partners for granted and either talk to them as if they were always listening (so there is no need to address them directly) or harbor so much resentment that we choke on saying their names and look elsewhere. Use your partner's name and use it often. Listen attentively, with your ears *and* your eyes. Refrain from making comments while your partner is sharing. No joking and no sarcasm. Be thoughtful and be kind, remembering that thoughtfulness is an elementary part of respect for your partner.

Activities

Make a copy of the statements and questions provided for your partner so you can complete them separately in your own notebooks. Allow ample time for this activity, but don't spend more than three or four minutes on each one or you will be at this activity for days instead of hours. Agree on a time to finish; then sit down together in a quiet, private place to share your answers, fill in the gaps, even make corrections.

1. **Hard Data—This Is What I Know about My Partner**
   Write down your partner's:
   Eye color; height; favorite food; favorite flower; favorite place; favorite film; favorite hobby, recreation or pastime; favorite place to dine; favorite book.

2. **My Goals, Needs and Memories**
   Answer the following about yourself, *not* your partner.
   A goal I have is...; Something I really need is...; My childhood was...

3. **My Hopes and Fears for Our Marriage**
   My greatest hope is ...; My greatest fear is...; I am most concerned about...; One reason I married you is...; I think our marriage is...

4. **Changes, Values and Pleasures**
   One thing I would like to change about myself is...; One thing I would like you to change is...; One thing I value is...; One thing I think you value is...; One thing I would like to do together is...; One thing I think you would like to do together is...

5. **Some Challenging Things to Share**
   My view of life is...; I think your view of life is...; My strengths are...; I think your strengths are...; My difficulties (weaknesses) are...; I think your difficulties (weaknesses) are...; I think (our, your, my) children are...

Come together and share your written responses with each other. Feel free to fill in the gaps or point out the differences and errors in perception. Remember to follow your Guidelines for Safe Communication. As you listen, be thoughtful and respond with kindness.

Sharing the Process
Now respond verbally to these questions together. Take turns and listen carefully, kindly and empathically.
- Did you share honestly and without reservation?
- Were there any surprises?
- What were the most significant things you learned?
- Is there anything you would like your partner to clear up?
- Did you feel any defensiveness when your partner shared? Just hear through the words to the feelings being expressed. You don't have

to fix it and you don't have to make it better. It is enough that you understand how your partner feels.

Appreciations
- Share one or two focused appreciations that flowed from your dialogue. And be sure to use *I* messages. For example: "When I got a little scared, I really appreciated you holding me and reassuring me that you are committed to this work."
- Share one way your partner is very special to you.

Close With—
- A warm embrace and a sincere "I love you."

Chapter 2

The Chaos of Disillusionment

Wisdom comes by disillusionment.
George Santayana

Oliver and Barbara Rose met at an estate auction, both in school on scholarships. They married. She waitressed and bore children while he finished law school and started climbing a law firm's ladder. He made it—big time. She located the perfect home, spent seven years transforming it and raised the kids while he socialized with clients. Finally, the house surpassed perfection, the children were off to Harvard and Barbara could not face spending the rest of her life with a man who had become a total stranger. She wanted out.

"Because," she told him, "when I watch you eat—when I see you asleep—when I look at you—lately—I just want to smash your face in."

Barbara filed for divorce, wanting only the house. Oliver decided *he* wanted the house. And so ensued a long and ugly battle which wiped out the pets, the Morgan automobile, Barbara's business, the house and, ultimately, the Roses themselves, who died entwined in the shattered chandelier on the prized terrazzo floor.

The War of the Roses, a 1981 novel by Warren Adler made into a 1989 film of the same name, is a satirical dig at just how wrong a marriage can go. While the plight of the Roses was severely exaggerated "Hollywood style," the real-life crumbling of a relationship exacts a tremendous toll on both parties and those whom they know.

Like the Roses' relationship, any marriage resting on a foundation of romantic illusion will have disastrous consequences. For each partner, it may lead to irresponsibility and the constant search for elusive fulfillment. For the children involved, it may lead to profound loss, internalized grief, anger and their attendant consequences. For society, it could mean the decay of the primary socializing unit—the family—and the subsequent propensity for increasing violence, abuse and alienation.

When one or both partners are entrenched in romantic illusions as the basis of the relationship, that relationship is destined to be an empty, unrewarding and compulsive search for the elixir of romance with its heady promise of enchantment. One couple I counseled had the serious problem of disillusionment that the film about the Roses highlighted.

Gwen and Lance met at a mutual friend's anniversary party and fell in love at first sight. They were sensible; they dated two years, were engaged for one more and then had a storybook wedding. They were the perfect couple—she an attractive nurse, he a successful entrepreneur. They each brought great hope and outstanding talent to the marriage. They also had an unwavering belief in the power of love to solve everything; their love would never die.

The daughter of an alcoholic father, Gwen was a workaholic, a perfectionist and quite self-critical. Lance, the son of a critical and punishing mother, worked hard, managed money well and tried very hard to please Gwen. Gwen's childhood script *(we'll be talking more about* scripts *in chapter 3) drove her to become hyper-critical of some of Lance's behaviors. Lance's childhood* script *drove him to believe that Gwen did not allow him to be himself. This repetitive pattern deterio-*

rated into anger, pain and verbal abuse. It blinded them to the very real contributions they both were bringing to the marriage. Neither could see how their family histories triggered behaviors and feelings.

Gwen and Lance love each other fully and are both deeply committed to the marriage. Their willingness to do something about their unhappiness brought them to counseling.

Despite friction and disillusionment, the many couples with whom I've worked successfully have proven that renewal as a couple is possible. Facing the challenge of working through issues offers an opportunity to refresh the marriage and to achieve increased intimacy, honesty, deeper understanding and a conscious and more effective communication as well as opportunities for sharing spiritual growth, giving and receiving genuine forgiveness and creating an enduring new bond.

When the darkness and chaos of disillusionment set in—and this happens in almost all long-term relationships—it is possible to decide that the relationship is worth the work and to move toward the creation of what we identified in chapter 1 as *intentional love*, which then becomes the key to a successful *intentional marriage*.

Intentional loving begins with thoughtful decisions you make every day. It requires taking responsibility for your own words, feelings and actions throughout the day. In order to act on the decision to create an intentional marriage, it will be crucial first to understand the individual development of every *person* and second to understand the developmental stages that every *couple* passes through.

Let's look first at the development of individuals, drawn from the work of Erik H. Erikson in *Childhood and Society*. Erikson believed that at every stage of life, people face what he called a psycho-social crisis, that is, a choice about how to develop. Our choices are influenced by the people and events in our individual lives. Infants, for example, learn to either trust or mistrust other people based on their early interactions with their caregivers.

If all goes well and these crises are resolved successfully, then it is possible to move forward to the next stage with the qualities and strengths accrued in the last. With those basic strengths, people are able to feel hope, to express will and individual choice, to focus upon a purpose, to have a sense of competence, to demonstrate fidelity, constancy, honesty and allegiance, to feel and express love, to be devoted, to care and to learn and generalize from life experiences.

Failure to resolve these crises successfully leads to pathological consequences including withdrawal, compulsion, inhibition, inertia, repudiation, exclusivity, disdain and disgust. An unsuccessful resolution at any stage will distort the emergence of the self at the next developmental stage and will impair all the developmental stages that follow.

The failure of an individual to develop has enormous consequences for a marriage. A marriage in which both partners have resolved these crises of development successfully will make the individual strong enough to move predictably through the progressive developmental stages of their marriage. A marriage wherein one or both partners have not successfully resolved their individual developmental tasks will face enormous challenges.

Just as individuals need to successfully navigate progressive stages of development in order to become mature, integrated adults, couples must successfully pass together through developmental stages. Success at each stage is based on the resolution of the previous one. A couple cannot evade, avoid or skip over a developmental stage. If this happens, a couple may remain stuck or *frozen* at one stage of development and one level of communication.

Now look at the five stages of couple development and see what you can recognize of your own relationship in them.

Stage 1: Romance

Each partner is dazzled and then blinded by the power of attraction. They gaze into each other's eyes and "see no difference, hear no difference, speak no difference." This is the stage wherein partners present their personas (how one wants to be seen) and hold back what they really hope for and expect. Hope and denial flow in equal portions and set up each partner for transition to Stage 2.

Stage 2: The Politics of Love

Romance sours with the first disillusionment and the relationship fills with disappointment. As partners turn to power as a substitute for love, a struggle for control emerges in some form and the emotional legacies of both partners' childhoods are introduced into the relationship. The *inner family theater* comes to life. (We will discuss the *inner family theater* in chapter 3.)

Couples in this stage are caught by paradoxical fears: the fear of engulfment, or loss of self, and the fear of abandonment. Intimacy as a couple and personal autonomy are experienced as mutually exclusive.

Each partner holds the other responsible for resolving the unmet emotional needs of the child he or she was in the past. Each feels, perhaps unconsciously, that his or her mate is responsible for his or her emotional well-being.

Stage 3: Disintegration

The relationship is characterized by continuing internal power struggles. A developmental crisis occurs when one partner, with either words or behavior, expresses an unwillingness to continue to live by the couple's unspoken emotional contract. Sometimes this is spawned by an event such as children growing up and moving out, the death of a child, a chronic or terminal illness, an affair or being forced into early retirement. Often this is characterized as "the mid-life crisis." Seeking resolution to the crisis, a person may fight with his or her partner, creating high drama, or take flight, escaping into work or an affair. None of these strategies allows productive resolution because the partners are not working through the crises together.

Stage 4: Rapprochement

This stage opens as partners seek to reestablish harmony in the relationship. Rapprochement specifically means the resumption of harmonious relations. This involves gaining the self-knowledge that supports understanding, forgiveness and reconciliation, plus a deep, genuine recommitment. The basis for mature love is established, but it requires learning new tools of communication that will support a new-found harmony.

Essential to this phase are forgiveness and acceptance, renewed courtship, the re-discovery of individual *selves* and learning to appreciate the special value of the other partner. Thus, mature love gains a foothold.

Stage 5: Devoted Love

In this stage, mature, active, intentional love can flourish. The vital force is love. Love is the glue that keeps the couple working and connected. Cohesion within the couple enables them to meet and survive the challenges and threats, both external and internal, to the relationship's existence. This couple lives the *principle of intentional love*. We will learn more about this in chapter 10.

As the couple's relationship matures, additional crises such as prolonged illness or disability come with aging, offering more opportunities for devotion, loyalty, patience and support. The full bloom of love's wisdom serves to sustain both partners.

In *The Art of Loving*, Erich Fromm describes a love that requires discipline, concentration, patience, faith and courage:

> *To love means to commit oneself without guarantee, to give oneself completely in the hope that our love will produce love in the loved person. Love is an act of faith, and whoever is of little faith is also of little love.*

Couples in Stage 5 make the decision to commit in this way every day.

If you are reading this book, chances are you find yourself in some degree of disillusionment about your relationship. You may have successfully transcended Stage 1 and be in Stage 2. Or perhaps you are stuck in Stage 3. The Endeavor following this chapter is designed to assist you in getting unstuck, so that you can experience the relief that comes with awareness and move forward.

Now that you have learned about developmental stages of individuals and couples, you are prepared to learn about the second concept crucial to the creation of a loving, intentional relationship: the *inner family theater*. Chapter 3 will help you to understand this *inner family theater* in yourself and your partner so that you can reach healthy and effective communication in your marriage or partnership.

Endeavor: Past as Prologue

Overview
The past profoundly impacts your present relationship. It can create barriers that interfere with how you get along with your partner or it can help you improve your marriage and enhance your connection. The latter is the goal of this Endeavor.

Activities
Find a comfortable, quiet place. One partner reads one sentence and responds and then the other partner reads the same sentence and responds. When both of you have completed the same sentence, proceed to the next, alternating who goes first.

Have your Guidelines for Safe Communications on hand and remember that kindness is paramount. Look at your partner directly, be receptive and non-judgmental. Don't interrupt and don't ask questions. If there are tears, you may touch or hold each other, but don't comment except with comforting body language.

1. **Thinking about You and Me**
    a. I feel excited by you when…
    b. I'd like to give you…
    c. I'm avoiding…
    d. What I love about you is…
    e. What I can forgive myself for is…
    f. What I forgive you for is…
    g. One way our marriage is appealing to me is…
    h. One way our marriage scares me is…
    i. What I would like to do for you that I am not now doing is…
    j. What I would like you to do for me that you are not now doing is…
    k. One difficulty I would like us to work on is…
    l. One way I contribute to our marriage is…

2. **Dialogue about Our Courtship and Other Memories**
   a. One thing I remember about our courtship that I really loved was...
   b. An early disappointment was... (Did I talk about it or did I just stuff it?)
   c. A time when I was upset with you was... (How was it resolved? Who made the first move toward making up?)
   d. Holidays, birthdays and anniversaries are... (Which ones are important? Does your partner remember which ones are important to you?)
   e. The part of our marriage ceremony I treasure most was...

3. **Make three requests of each other based on your disclosures and agree to do at least one or more of the other's requests.** Write these in your notebooks.

Sharing the Process
   - Did you use your Guidelines for Safe Communication?
   - Did you share honestly and without reservation? Any hesitations?
   - Were there any surprises?
   - What were the most significant things you learned?
   - Is there anything you would like your partner to clear up?
   - Do you remember the same things in different ways?

Appreciations
Remember to use eye contact; listen carefully; do not interrupt or answer the appreciations. A simple "thank you" will do as a response. No sarcasm, teasing or joking.
   - Share one or two focused appreciations of your partner that flow from your shared dialogue.
   - Share one way your partner is special to you. Be specific.
   - Share one thing your partner said that had special meaning for you.

Close With—
- A long hug and an authentic "I love you."

Chapter 3

The Inner Family Theater

The inside always manifests itself on the outside.
Confucius

Before you begin the work needed to realize the loving relationship everyone deserves, it is necessary to understand a concept called the *inner family theater*. As Eric Berne has described in many of his books, people bring hidden *scripts* into relationships. These *scripts* are peopled by the characters and plotted with the events of our childhoods. Together, these people, plots and events comprise our *inner family theater*.

When we are children, our main task is learning how to survive among the giants who rule our lives (parents, older siblings, aunts, uncles or other significant figures in our immediate surroundings). We depend upon these people for our sustenance and nurturing. To survive among these powerful giants, we internalize messages from them that tell us how to get along, avoid punishment, be appreciated and obtain what we need but cannot yet supply for ourselves. We receive instructions about how to behave and how to be. We internalize these instructions as *do*s and *don't*s, *should*s, *must*s, *ought*s, *can* or *can't do*s, *can* or *can't be*s and so on. In response to these internalized messages, we make decisions about who we are and how we will behave. We make these key decisions early in life, usually before we are four or five years old. Then we forget them; that is, we push them out of our awareness. In effect, we hide them from ourselves. These internalized messages then become the inner talk and hidden decisions that rule our lives.

The inner talk and hidden decisions form a life plan called a *script*. A s*cript* is the set of guidelines a person created to survive emotionally in his or her childhood and is anchored in the unconscious. Simply stated, we live by the s*cripts* we chose as a young child.

A person's *script* is both taught by reward or punishment of early behaviors and reinforced throughout life or until it is interrupted and changed. It drives a person blindly until he or she understands it and takes action to change it. Our job, as adults, is to learn about our own *scripts* and change them so we can live lives that are truly our own— lives not run by messages from the past.

A parent who is too indulgent, for example, fails to provide a child with the skills to survive as an adult. At the other extreme, a parent who is not understanding enough incapacitates the child. These are the dramas of childhood from which we make the decisions that determine our *scripts*. We bring our *scripts* into our adult lives, because they are familiar and comfortable. And so we are loyal to these ancient *script* decisions—to the plots and players of our *inner family theaters*. The choices we made as children now create the plots we incorporate into our lives as adults. For most of us, this theater is hidden from our consciousness. The play unfolds and the actors act, with our partners as the unwitting participants or audience.

No wonder we are dismayed when our marriages seem to be turning out to be just like or just the opposite of our parents' marriages. No wonder a couple is surprised when their marriage loses its romance and is experienced as unrewarding, unsatisfying, even abusive. It is the *inner family theater* within each partner that is activated in the conversations, conflicts and arguments of the relationship.

When a couple argues, they draw upon words and concepts they've learned in the past that are calculated to wound and hurt. These words are intended to reach the most vulnerable part of the opponent and usually fall into one of three categories: attack, blame or defense. Often each partner has spent a long time learning his opponent's weakest and most vulnerable places. Sarcasm, yelling, withdrawal and a variety of other aggressive, passive-aggressive and debasing tactics are calculated to wound and to win. These arguments are all too often recycled again and again, because neither partner has any consciousness of the underlying drivers to these painful encounters. Gwen and Lance, a couple brought up in an earlier chapter were a seemingly perfect pair whose storybook, love-at-first-sight romance descended into a repetitive pattern of criticism and verbal abuse. Their recycled argument looks like this:

> Gwen: "Sometimes I feel like I live in a men's gym, Lance. Why do you insist on leaving bath towels on the floor all the time?"
>
> Lance: "Geez, Gwen, it's not all the time. So I get in a hurry sometimes—you are so anal it makes me crazy! Lighten up!"
>
> Gwen: "You just don't get it, do you? Like that derelict brother of yours. You just can't see that his irresponsibility will drive your company into the ditch. That scares the heck out of me, Lance."
>
> Lance: "Don't start with my brother, Gwen. You know, sometimes you can be so selfish."
>
> Gwen: "Oh, so I'm the selfish one now? All I'm trying to do is save your business so we can have some kind of reasonable life."
>
> Lance: "I'm perfectly capable of running my own business, Gwen. And leave my family out of it! Oh, forget it, I'm out of here."
>
> Gwen: "Great, go ahead. This is what you always do, Lance. Well, fine—I can rear our unborn child by myself. I don't need you and guess what: I can be out of here before you come back tonight."

The real characters in this oft-repeated struggle are not Gwen and Lance. In Gwen's criticism, Lance hears his critical, punishing mother. In Lance's messiness (and especially when he walks out the door to have a beer with his friends) Gwen sees her alcoholic father. Lance's and Gwen's *inner family theaters* furnished the stage for this escalating and repetitive struggle. The *scripts* were written a long time ago. How were those *scripts* written? Who takes the speaking role? How are the dynamics of this drama determined? Before we can answer these questions, we must understand the important role of *projection* in these family arguments.

Projection is a law of life. Defined, projection is the act of attributing, or splitting off, an unwanted part of ourselves onto another person and then reacting to that part as separate from ourselves. The clearest analogy is to a movie projector. The crucial elements—film, light and lenses—are inside the apparatus, but the image is cast outside onto a screen to create the appearance of an external reality. In the same way, our reality is what we project outward onto the screen of the other. We see ourselves in others and since it is the disowned and least likable parts of us we are seeing, we react with varying degrees of anger and fear. Once we understand the operations of projection, then we can begin to examine the source. For partners in troubled relationships, that source is the *inner family theater.*

We accumulate, in infancy and childhood, a variety of defense mechanisms that conflicted partners often use in their arguments and misunderstandings in some combination. Some of them are useful, important and helpful. Some of them are dysfunctional blocks to healthy living and need to be removed in order to encourage healthy emotional growth and lasting love. If you and your mate want to gain a true, loving, lasting relationship, our goal in working together will be to first understand the operation of certain key defense mechanisms in yourselves and your relationship.

Key Defenses
1. **Denial** – painful, anxiety-producing thoughts are screened out.
2. **Introjection** – another person's or group's behaviors are incorporated into an individual's personality.

3. **Projection** – unacceptable impulses and thoughts are attributed to others or personal failures are blamed on others. These patterns are often used to justify prejudice or to evade responsibility.
4. **Idealization** – positive attributes in the other are exaggerated, either consciously or unconsciously, and imperfections or failings in the other are disregarded; the other appears perfect or nearly perfect.
5. **Regression** – reversion to immature behavior when threatened with overwhelming external problems or internal conflicts.
6. **Reaction Formation** – unacceptable or threatening impulses are denied by going to the opposite extreme.
7. **Sublimation** – unacceptable sexual or aggressive drives are channeled into acceptable expression.
8. **Intellectualization** – emotional problems are dealt with abstractly or by excessive intellectual activity.
9. **Rationalization** – questionable reasons are given to justify unacceptable behavior or personal shortcomings to ward off guilt, maintain self-respect and avoid criticism.

Derived from the *inner family theater*, these defenses are created when we internalize key messages from the all-important people in our childhoods and are organized outside our conscious awareness. If, as adults, we become aware of who is doing the thinking, the talking and the acting, we then can become aware of who is running the show, meaning *our words, our actions and our lives.* How can we cultivate this awareness? First, by recognizing the key players common to all *inner family theaters.*

Each person's *inner family theater* is arranged differently, with the key players in the dialogues exchanging the lead from time to time depending upon how our inner emotions are triggered. When an inner player on our stage is triggered, he or she reacts impulsively, without thought, and uses projections to attack, blame or defend. This frequently escalates as other characters on the inner stage get involved. Then the adrenaline pump really gets going. The pulse rises and the inner players' feelings begin to show in the way the body feels, looks and moves. These are called *somatic* effects—the way in which our bodies reveal our emotional state.

Who are the key characters on the inner stage? Recognizing them will be useful as you learn to change the inner family *scripts* that keep you trapped and unhappy as you strive to gain lasting love.

The Natural Child – This character is totally open to all inner and outer experiences. As children, human beings are playful, spontaneous, intuitive, creative and impulsive. The natural child is the child who loved to play, to have fun and to be alive. In your adult life, this is the writer, the artist, the poet, the musician, the dancer—the creative aspect of yourself.

The Not OK Child – This player represents the part of yourself that was often repressed, penalized and punished. This inner aspect may have made decisions as a result of some trauma or series of traumas you sustained as a child, now tucked away out of consciousness. The Not OK Child hides away for no one to see, for the child may have been punished or ridiculed and fears showing himself. Inviting, feeding and thriving on put-down messages, the Not OK Child believes the inner, critical self-talk he hears and feels helpless, rejected, picked on, unworthy, guilty, ashamed, lonely, ignored, rebellious, bad, deprived, worthless, unacceptable and unloved.

Your Inner Parents

Whoever took care of you when you were a child impacted your behavior, thoughts and feelings in significant, often dramatic ways. You studied every aspect of them and gradually pulled them in, learned their words, gestures, facial expressions. These caretaker messages make up the Nurturing Parent and the Critical Parent.

The Nurturing Parent – Children learn nurturing messages when parents and caretakers model constructive, healthy attitudes. When they were trustworthy, nonjudgmental, empathic, comforting and supportive, your caretakers reinforced a good basic sense of yourself. Characteristics of good nurturing include being appreciative and supportive, keeping suggestions and requests reasonable and possible, in line with what a child could handle at the time. Nurturing parents respond to physical and psychological needs with understanding and cooperation within a reasonable time. They demonstrate how to love and be loved unconditionally. This does not mean they support everything the child does. They separate the child they love from the actions of which they disapprove and communicate this in a firm, understanding manner.

The Critical Parent – Critical Parent messages are taught to children consciously and unconsciously by any number of others, including older siblings, aunts, uncles, authority figures, teachers, the media, neighbors. In all of these people, there are two aspects—the Nurturing Parent and the Critical Parent. Critical Parent messages may also be taught by an abusive, punishing, neglectful or exploiting parent.

The Critical Parent discounts the child's feelings and intuition and teaches the child to look outside himself or herself for approval and control. They have little faith in the child and assert that what they do is *for the child's own good*. They focus on what is wrong with the child, what is missing. When every misstep is criticized and punished, a child learns that his or her sense of self depends on what he or she does and not on who he or she intrinsically is.

Whatever Critical Parent messages you received in childhood created the inner character who judges, scolds, shames, criticizes, punishes, deprives, blames, attacks, finds fault with and rejects you. Characteristics of the inner Critical Parent are over-control, impossible demands and over-strictness, with too many *should*s, *ought*s, *must*s, *have to*s, *don't*s and *cannot*s.

There is a direct connection between the Critical Parent messages internalized as a child and the inner Not OK Child in the *inner family theater*. When adults are exposed to Critical Parent messages, the Not OK Child reemerges and triggers those old feelings, causing low self-esteem. The messages we give ourselves through this collusion between the inner Critical Parent and the inner Not OK Child contain self-blame, self-judgments, self-discounts, shame and injunctions. The amount of Not OKness a person lives with now derives directly from the amount of criticism, control or neglect he or she lived with then.

The Nurturing Parent and Natural Child inner messages are concerned with love. The Critical Parent and Not OK Child are concerned with power. These are the primary players in the *inner family theater*. A good rule of thumb is to remember that *where power rules, love perishes*. So it will be imperative to identify the Nurturing Parent and Natural Child within yourself and make sure they take center stage most of the time.

Now let's discover who is on stage:

In the *scripts* people put together as children, we assign parts of us the role of *choosers*. Choosers house the feelings we have toward ourselves and also determine who is on stage. The choices of a person who dislikes or judges himself or herself will be dominated by deep discontent. His or her stage will be occupied by the Tempestuous Child; Unruly, Rebellious Child; Victim or Martyr Child; Cynical or Ashamed Child; Guilty or Doubting Child; Condemning or Condemned Child. Whoever occupies the stage determines how an individual will respond to any given situation, so the chooser controls a person's face, body, expressions and reactions.

In any relationship, both partners carry the hidden, internalized aspects of their childhoods. Once there is a commitment between them, each partner expects the other to fulfill the unmet needs of childhood, while at the same time the ghosts of internalized parents emerge and despoil communication.

You can break free of this cast of characters and learn to distinguish between feelings, responses and behaviors triggered by your *inner family theater* and those that are grounded in the reality of the here and now. You do not have to use old, neurotic solutions to alleviate present, legitimate suffering.

Gaining consciousness of the many aspects of your *inner family theater* is the first essential step in knowing who occupies center stage and how your inner actors are triggered. Once you reach this awareness, you will have the power of choice to be a prisoner of your *script* or to release the grasp it has. You can choose the aspects of your inner being that you wish to keep and release the rest.

A distinctive marital dance that is *script-driven* links two partners in a seemingly endless succession of transactions that disclose a psychological arrangement between them. For our purposes, this dance will be called the *marital melodrama*.

If you are to release the repetitive *marital melodrama* that characterizes your relationship conflict, it is essential that both you and your partner understand three aspects of your *inner family theaters*. First, who are the actors and who takes the stage most of the time? Second, what is the emotional aspect of each actor; knowing this, you can begin to understand your triggers and projections. Third, how can you take responsibility for these actors, triggers and messages, so you do not react blindly and thoughtlessly? This requires that you come from a place of awareness, thoughtfulness, kindness and understanding of yourself and your partner.

In the two Endeavors that follow this chapter, "Who Wrote This Thing?" and "Curtain Up," you and your partner will discover the *scripts* you wrote in early childhood. You will identify the actors, their emotions, your triggers and projections and other defenses. You will learn to notice the times when you and your partner shift into *marital melodrama*, where your *scripts* run the show. Each of you must work to create new ideas and ways of responding that will help you release the repetitive pattern that creates such conflicts so that you may transcend your childhood *scripts* and build a truly autonomous, reciprocally rewarding relationship capable of nurture, intimacy and love.

Endeavor: Who Wrote This Thing?

Overview

As chapter 2 explains, you wrote your own *script* during infancy and childhood and still carry it with you today. Most adults are unaware of their *scripts*. By exploring your own *script*, sharing your insights with your partner and learning about your partner's *script*, you can begin to recognize and pay attention to the times when you and your partner shift into the *marital melodrama*—that is, any scene, discussion or argument wherein your *scripts* (either one partner's or both) are running the show.

The actors in your *script* include your Inner Mother (or mother substitute), who may be some combination of mean, abusive, rejecting, benign, loving or caring; your Inner Father, who may be some combination of supportive, loving, critical, abusive, absent or uninvolved; and your Inner Child, who had to figure out how to survive. This Inner Child may be angry, afraid, withdrawn, needy, sad, ashamed, hurt, bewildered, hungry for acceptance and love and other aspects that become character attributes in later life. Sometimes there is a healthy, free Inner Child, but there is almost always a child who *hopes* to be free, accepted and loved.

As you do these activities, see if you can *hear* the inner voices from a *script* you wrote a long time ago that continue to control your responses.

Activities

Take as much time as you need to answer the next questions. Do not be too concerned if there are things you can't remember—write down only what comes readily to mind. Remember, this is not a test that you pass or fail. Answering the questionnaire will help you become familiar with those aspects of your childhood that impact your choices and actions today. Be sure you and your partner have separate copies. Take some time by yourselves and answer the questions in individual notebooks. When you both have completed answering all the questions, get together and share the answers.

Learning About Your Script

A. Just the Facts

Date today... ; date of birth... ; present age... ; your birth order...; number of younger brothers... ; number of older brothers... ; number of younger sisters... ; number of older sisters... ; names, ages and whether they are living or deceased (include all of your siblings—full, half, adopted and step).

1. Are you single, married, separated, divorced, widowed? Prior marriage(s)? If yes, how many and how long?
2. When you were an infant and child, who were the significant adults in your life?
3. Any significant death(s) affecting your life? (accident, illness, suicide, murder)
4. Children (names, ages and whether they are living at home, including full, adopted, step)

B. About My Name

Am I named after someone? What are my nicknames? What was I called as a child? From where does my family (maiden) name come? (heritage and ancestry)

C. Childhood Memories

When I was a child, this was my favorite—

Comic strip; song; story; fairy tale; book; hero/heroine; legend; movie; television program; other...

Significant childhood events—

1. Did I ever have a serious accident?
2. Was I ashamed of anything?
3. What was I afraid of?
4. Was I ever in trouble?
5. Was I ever seriously ill? Any surgery?
6. Did my parents drink alcohol? Use drugs?
7. What do I remember about my grandparents?

8. What is the saddest thing I remember about my childhood?
9. What was the happiest moment(s) of my childhood?
10. What bothered me most as a child?
11. Did I wonder how I would end up?

D. **Parental Messages**
1. When I was a small child, what did my parents and/or influential adults say to me? (first thought)
2. How was I nurtured as a child? By mother? By father? Others?
3. How was I criticized? By mother? By father? Others?
4. How was I punished? By whom?
5. To whom was I compared?
6. What did my parents say at the dinner table?
7. What did they do when the "going got tough?"
8. What do I remember about my mother? (first thought)
9. What do I remember about my father? (first thought)
10. What problems or "hang-ups" did they have?
11. Was there anything I was afraid of? Did I panic?

E. **Key Impacts of Parental Messages on My Life**
1. One decision I made early in life is...
2. What did they tell me I should do? What did they tell me I should be?
3. What did they tell me I shouldn't do? What did they tell me I shouldn't be?
4. What do I really want to do and be?
5. How do I think I will screw it up, do it wrong or fail because of these early communications?
6. One thing I feel these messages have given me permission to do is...
7. A *don't be* message was...
8. Things will be different when...
9. What happens when things go well?
10. What happens when things go wrong?
11. My main problem is...

F. **Later in Life**
   1. What will I do or be in my later years?
   2. At what age do I expect to die?
   3. How did I come to pick that age?
   4. What will be put on my tombstone? (or memorial block, urn)
   5. What will be put on my partner's tombstone? (or memorial block, urn)

Now get together with your partner and share your answers, taking turns, one section at a time. Use your Guidelines for Safe Communication. As each one shares, simply listen to your partner's answers. Do not comment. Do not be judgmental, teasing or joking in any way. Give your partner your full attention; take brief notes if you need to, so that you later can ask focused questions to get more clarity. Simply ask for more information and be sure not to ask why questions. A why question puts your listener on the defensive.

Sharing the Process
Answer these questions out loud together.
- What are three things you learned about yourself?
- What are three things you learned about your partner?
- Did this exercise bring any awareness to you about how you behave toward your partner?
- What would you like to change in yourself as a result of the awareness you gained from this Endeavor?

Appreciations
Again, remember, partners should use eye contact, listen carefully to each other and not interrupt or answer the appreciations.
- Share one or two specific appreciations about your partner that flow from your work together in this Endeavor.
- Express appreciation for one way your partner's sharing was important to you. Be specific; be kind.

Close With—
- Give your partner a smile, a hug and a thank you for loving you enough to do this work!

Endeavor: Curtain Up

Overview

You have identified the elements of the *script* you wrote as a child. Now it is time to learn how your *script* becomes operable as an adult during your *marital melodrama*. This exercise is all about learning how *we are all loyal to the pain of our childhoods*. What you learned in childhood is brought into your adult life, where you blindly relive it over and over again. This Endeavor will help you to recognize when the curtain goes up and your *scripts* are running the show. Later, we'll learn new ideas and behaviors to overcome *scripts* and bring down the curtain on repetitive, painful and destructive *marital melodramas*.

Activities

Find a couple of quiet spots where you and your partner can separately read and reflect on the following concepts. As always, you will each need a copy of the material. As you read through these concepts, reflect on how they might apply to your life. Make notes when you discover any insights or "aha" moments.

When you have finished, get together and share your reflections. Be sure to follow the Guidelines for Safe Communication. Each of you should listen attentively and ask questions to help increase your understanding. Ask without judgment and with care and empathy. Remember not to ask *why* questions, comment, tease, mock or make fun of your partner's reflections.

1. **Preliminary Concepts and Information**
   What Every *Script* Contains:
   1. A *storyline/theme* – gives meaning to your life's choices
   2. A *cast of characters* – made up of the people in your *inner family theater*
   3. A *key decision* – made early in life, this determines how you react in your *marital melodrama*
   4. A *set of key defenses* – used to maintain your *script* and your *marital melodrama*
   5. A *basic life position* – your sense of your own "OKness"

2. The Four Primary *Scripts* (as described by Claude Steiner in *Scripts People Live: Transactional Analysis of Life Scripts*):

    Joylessness: Taught by the spoken or unspoken commands, demands and expectations of childhood. A key decision may be "I have no right to be happy and I make other people unhappy by my behavior" or "I am just like my (drunken father or angry mother)."

    Mindlessness: Taught by the disregard or overlooking of your intelligence that you experienced as a child. A key decision may be "I am stupid, a failure or just plain dumb."

    Lovelessness: Taught by those who withheld their love, approval and authentic praise of you as a child. If you do not receive appreciation, you are not able to give appreciation and gratitude to others. A key decision may be "I am unworthy, unlovable or unloved as I am," so "I must be good" or "I will be bad." Both of these bring counterfeit substitutes for love.

    Powerlessness: Taught by caregivers who were unable to be powerful themselves. These include parents whose behavior involved blaming and attacking their children and defending themselves. Sometimes, parents and children switch roles, becoming either *helpers,* to avoid feeling guilty, or *victims*, because they feel resentful. Up against this, children make key decisions such as "I am Not OK and I must please others to get them to like me;" "I will be hurt by others unless I please them;" "I am bad, so I will get even."

3. Discovering More About Your *Script*

    Now that you have read about the concepts that underlie *scripts*, create your *script* story by responding to the following:

    a. Theme: What was the name and theme of the fairy tale or story you loved most as a child? The theme could be about love, hate, gratitude or revenge. For example, in Rapunzel, a fairy tale about a young girl who uses her long hair to reach her prince, the theme involves love and sacrifice. *Identify the theme of your story.*

b. **Life Positions:**
   Identify the one that rings truest for you as your life position.
   1. I'm OK; you're OK.
   2. I'm OK; you're not OK.
   3. I'm not OK; you're OK.
   4. I'm not OK; you're not OK.

c. **Key Decision:** Choose one from the examples below or construct one that fits you best. For example, when I was young, I was spanked with a wooden spoon whenever my mother was angry and upset with me, so I decided "I can't be me. I have to be a good boy."
   - I am not lovable.
   - If I don't behave in a certain way, I will be abandoned.
   - If I don't hide the real me, I will be engulfed.
   - I do not have a right to be.
   - I am a failure.
   - I can't be me. I have to be...
   - I am hated.
   - I can never have what I want.
   - I cannot be what I want to be.
   - I have to be perfect.
   - It's never enough.
   - I must always please.

   Describe in your notebook an event in your childhood that illustrates your key decision.

d. **Supporting Decision:** What other decisions did you make to support your key decision? Pick the one sentence fragment that rings truest for you or create one that is a better fit. Then write about it in your notebook. Here are some possible helpful insights:
   - I will be...; then I will be loved.
   - I will be perfect; then I will be...
   - I have to be in control, because...

- I will be a star to please...
- I will never cry, because...
- I will be beautiful, then I will be...
- I must please others, because...
- I'll never show my feelings, because...

For example: "I will be perfect all the time; then I will be noticed and loved and not be criticized or yelled at."

Identify what your supporting decision was.

e. **Double Binds:** A double bind occurs when the Critical Parent message in your head contradicts or blocks what your Inner Free Child would like. This prevents you, as an adult, from taking the constructive action required to be effective, loving and responsible. When what you want to say or do is blocked by your double bind, it usually leads to a headache—sometimes very severe. *What is your double bind?*

f. **Permissions/Protections:** Permissions are messages that allow you to feel good and positive about yourself and engage in activities that you really enjoy, e.g., do something creative, play an instrument or participate in a sport. Protections are messages that warn against danger, such as wash your hands, brush your teeth, don't run into the street.
Identify and write about your Permissions...
Identify and write about your Protections...

g. **The Internal Release (the spell-breaker):** This is an event or moment that lifts the commands and directives of childhood and frees us to fulfill our own autonomous aspirations. This internal release may be either event-centered or time-centered. A time-centered spell-breaker: "You can be independent and do what you want to do when you reach your eighteenth birthday—until then you have to follow our rules."
What was or is your time-centered spell-breaker?

An event-centered spell-breaker: "When you have completed college and obtained a job, you can then be free to do whatever you want."
What was or is your event-centered spell-breaker?

h. **The Four Primary** *Scripts*: Select one or more and write about it in your notebook.
1. *Joylessness* – Recall the commands, demands and injunctions you received as a child.
2. *Mindlessness* – Recall the ways you were discounted as a child.
3. *Lovelessness* – Recall the ways you were taught that you were not lovable and that your love was not acceptable.
4. *Powerlessness* – Recall the ways you could not express yourself as a child.

(More information about how *scripts* work may be found in *Games People Play* by Eric Berne.) It is important to know that we are attached to our particular *scripts*. We may not like them, but they are familiar, so we will choose to behave in a manner that invites these feelings to return over and over again.

4. **Transcending Your** *Script* **Is Possible!**
A person supported by a loving partner, an enlightened friend or caring therapist may alter, modify, rewrite or transcend his or her *script* to become an authentic, joyful, fully loving and fully living human being.

In your individual notebook…
- Write down what you want to change about your *script*.
- Identify some concrete and specific steps you will take to accomplish this.

Now get together and share your *script* material with your partner. Take turns and read one section at a time. Remember to use your Guidelines for Safe Communication.

Sharing the Process
These are to be read and answered together.
- What specifically did you learn from this exercise?
- What did you learn about yourself that was unexpected?
- What did you learn about your partner that you did not expect?
- What was helpful to you as you learned about your *script*?
- What was helpful to you as you learned about your partner's *script*?

Appreciations
Again, use eye contact, listen carefully and do not interrupt or answer the appreciations except for a heartfelt "thank you" at the end.
- Share one or two focused appreciations for your partner that flowed from his or her sharing.

Close With—
- a heartfelt hug and a grateful "I love you."

A Final Activity
Go on a date when you complete this Endeavor and celebrate how far you have come and how much you have learned about yourself, your partner and your marriage. Notice the special closeness that comes with dedication and the kind of commitment you both are making to this process.

Chapter 4

The Crossroads:
Taking up the Challenge

*The diamond cannot be polished without
friction, nor the man perfected without trials.*
Chinese Proverb

The only relationship that works is one on which we work. This should be your and your partner's mantra as we work through the tasks ahead. As I said in the beginning of this book, love is a decision we make every day. A committed and loving connection with a chosen partner is obtained by a *conscious intention* to work on the relationship and commit to these preconditions:

Release the search for the ideal partner.

Realize that by saying the one *yes* to your partner, you say a million *no*s to all other possibilities.

Give up the emotional rights, expectations and demands you once *required* from your partner.

Surrender the need to change the other and the hope and expectation that the other will change or that you can make him or her change.

Consciously and intentionally commit to creating an aware and rewarding partnership.

Commit to work on the relationship; realize that **the only relationship that works is one on which we work.**

Having taken up the challenge, let's review the developmental stages in a couple's life, introduced in chapter 2, allowing these basic tenets to guide us:

1. A couple's relationship metamorphoses through a progression of regular, fixed developmental stages that cannot be skipped or omitted.
2. Early childhood development profoundly impacts coupled relationships.
3. Each stage in a couple's life has specific developmental tasks to be accomplished and requires new skills based upon the transformation that occurred in the preceding stage.
4. When a couple is unable to progress through these stages, the developmental process is interrupted and developmental arrest occurs. Mild to severe difficulties will emerge in their relationship.
5. Each developmental stage contains a transitional crisis that, if successfully solved, will forward the couple to the next stage. This crisis is a time of both *danger* and *opportunity*. The *danger* is that if not solved constructively, the crisis will contribute to the stagnation, decline or demise of the relationship. The *opportunity* is for greater growth, increased awareness and advancement to the next stage.
6. Information, guidance and interventions can be designed to help couples move through the difficulties they encounter in each developmental stage of their journey.

Keeping these tenets in mind, let's explore each stage in a couple's development in more detail. Figures 1–5 offer a convenient view of the five stages of a couple's development, with their attendant emotional characteristics, communication styles, transitional crises and challenges. The hope is that you and your partner will recognize yourselves in the emotions of each stage, become willing to work through the crisis and then choose to communicate in a more honest and loving way, so that progression to the next stage can be made successfully. A scenario from the lives of real couples is given to illustrate each of the five stages, beginning with an example of a couple who are in Stage 1.

Figure 1: Stage 1: Romance

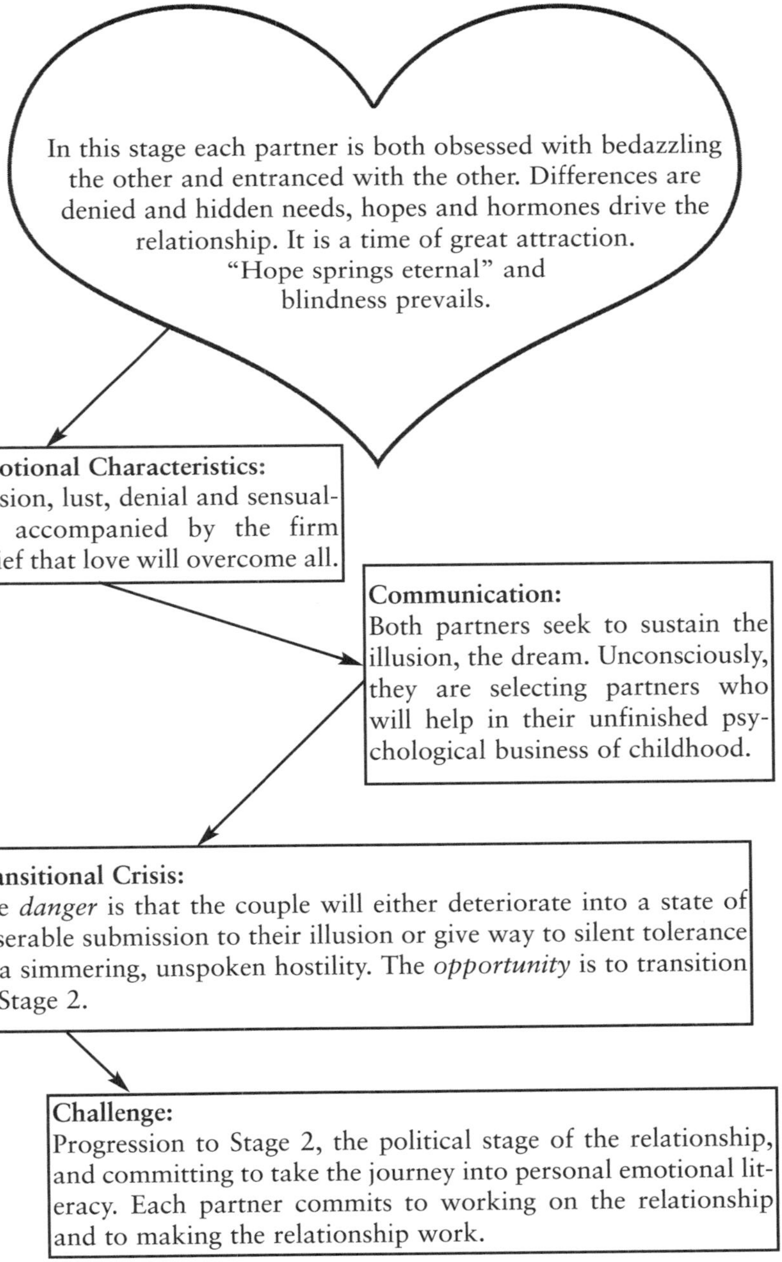

In this stage each partner is both obsessed with bedazzling the other and entranced with the other. Differences are denied and hidden needs, hopes and hormones drive the relationship. It is a time of great attraction.
"Hope springs eternal" and
blindness prevails.

Emotional Characteristics:
Illusion, lust, denial and sensuality, accompanied by the firm belief that love will overcome all.

Communication:
Both partners seek to sustain the illusion, the dream. Unconsciously, they are selecting partners who will help in their unfinished psychological business of childhood.

Transitional Crisis:
The *danger* is that the couple will either deteriorate into a state of miserable submission to their illusion or give way to silent tolerance or a simmering, unspoken hostility. The *opportunity* is to transition to Stage 2.

Challenge:
Progression to Stage 2, the political stage of the relationship, and committing to take the journey into personal emotional literacy. Each partner commits to working on the relationship and to making the relationship work.

> *Rob responded to Andrea's advertisement in the "connec-*
> *tions" section of the local paper and they immediately fell in*
> *love. They dated, became intimate and seemed the perfect*
> *match for each other. They enjoyed doing the same things;*
> *each seemed vitally interested in the other; they were affection-*
> *ate; they were good friends. But romance, you remember, is in*
> *the "eye of the beholder." Each was seeing what he or she*
> *wanted to see in the other and could not look at the other's*
> *"shadow." Blinded by the romantic delusion of what she*
> *thought she saw, Andrea did not know that Rob was having*
> *an affair with her best friend. She could not see that he was*
> *lying, drinking, smoking pot and conniving to get her to pay*
> *off his debts. When the reality of these behaviors became too*
> *clear to deny, Andrea felt deeply wounded, saying Rob had*
> *betrayed her noble belief in trust and love. Her belief in the*
> *myth that love conquers all drove Andrea blindly on, exacting*
> *promises from a tearful Rob that he would change his ways.*

In this couple, we can see all the emotional characteristics of Stage 1 (see Figure 1). They entered into a crisis when Andrea discovered Rob's substance abuse, affair and lies. We will find out later whether or not they were able to face the challenge, change their behaviors and successfully transition into Stage 2.

There may be a long interlude, sometimes many years, for couples in Stage 2 when the differences that seethe in the beginning of the stage seemingly give way to a settled relationship. In this resolution, both partners settle for what they have, even though it may be conflicting, unsatisfying, even boring. This period of submission can be character- ized by lovelessness, joylessness and powerlessness. The partners sup- press their differences and their own needs and desires. They reach unspoken emotional contracts, accepted roles for each other and settled understandings derived from struggles about such things as chores, money, children, holidays, vacations. This is the time when children are born and raised, homes are bought and the American Dream is sought. It may last a few years, many years or even a lifetime.

Figure 2: Stage 2: The Politics of Love

Partners are no longer willing to fully please each other. Each begins to assert what "I need." Self-assertion grows; disappointment in each other increases; romance sours. Fights more and more chatacterize the relationship. Disillusionment arises. Power struggles emerge. These may be continuous or intermittent with times of truces and seeming quiescence.

Emotional Characteristics:
Conflict, projection, projective identification and alternating imbalance of power. The struggle takes on the dynamics of the partners' *inner family theaters* in a blind way; disappointment, hurt, anger, bewilderment and confusion reign supreme. The magic and mystery of love have let them down. Romance's promise has been broken.

Communication:
Script-driven power struggles, arguments, bickering, conflict, m i s u n d e r s t a n d i n g . Communication is driven by the triggers of accusations, blame and defenses that hurt, wound and further disinte-grate the promise of romance.

Transitional Crisis:
The *danger* is that the partners will eventually withdraw from the conflict, resigning themselves to the "way things are." Boredom and silent hostility can result. *Couples can get stuck in this stage for many years—even for the duration of the marriage.*

Challenge:
Partners take responsibility for their own emotional lives and communcation, transcending the attack, blame and defend game; they refrain from using sarcasm and name-calling and learn to decode the language of their *inner family actors*. The *opportunity* is to continue the commitment to each other, to the task of becoming emotionally literate and progressing to Stage 3.

Here is a couple stranded in the more negative characteristics of Stage 2 (see Figure 2).

> *Betsy and Link met when she was an effervescent Elvis Presley fan and he a handsome naval officer. Theirs was a hot, romantic, passionate love affair that culminated in marriage and soon they had a beautiful little girl. Over time, Link became a fairly successful businessman, while Betsy went to school and earned multiple degrees. But the romantic bliss they both believed would sustain them forever soon deteriorated into rage, withdrawal and pain.*
>
> *Betsy had an angry father, who taught her well how to use angry words as weapons. Link, whose mother withheld her love and respect from him "for his own good," sought in Betsy the love and respect he'd been denied. When Betsy attacked Link, he did what he learned to do as a child: he withdrew. This behavior only fed Betsy's rage and she attacked him even more, which, of course, only prompted Link to hide more. Betsy began to smoke and overeat. They remained stuck in this repetitive and escalating trap for years.*

An Important Word about Alcohol and Drugs

Couples can get stuck in Stage 2 indefinitely and the use of alcohol or drugs is often the reason. Any relationship that includes substance abuse has two strikes against it. Firstly, the abuse clouds perceptions and hinders clear understanding of the self, the partner and the dynamics of the marriage. Secondly, the abuse fuels the *marital melodrama* by lowering inhibitions, loosening the tongue and lubricating emotions during discussions and arguments. Resentments long harbored are given full voice.

One of the most pervasive symptoms of addiction is denial. Persons in the grip of alcohol or drugs will often deny there is a problem. They will use anything in their inventory to protect their continued abuse—including blame, attack and elaborate defenses.

In a relationship where alcohol and/or drugs are used to excess by one or both of the partners, it is imperative to seek and get help for that problem first. No relationship can withstand the struggle for the heart and mind of the marriage if it also includes a struggle with alcohol and/or drugs.

The transition to Stage 3 is usually triggered by a life-altering event which challenges the unspoken emotional contract. When one of the partners decides he or she is no longer willing to live by that unspoken emotional contract, the shift to Stage 3 begins.

Look at Figure 3, Stage 3: Disintegration.

Bruce and Nancy illustrate one outcome of a Stage 3 relationship. They are a talented, hard-working, dedicated couple—each fully believing in the romantic fictions identified in chapter 1. They accumulated property and began building toward their family's comfortable future. Yet something went exceedingly wrong. Unrealistic expectations led them to demand too much from each other and from the marriage. High hopes were dashed and the childhood scripts from their respective inner family theaters took over. Soon anger increased, betrayal hovered and the marriage became mired in blame, attack and defense games. Fueled by alcohol, this melodrama turned to tragedy. A tragedy differs from a melodrama in that the actors in the tragedy end up in the courtroom, the morgue or the hospital. This one took its battle into divorce court, where they fought over every comma, every period, every piece of property—all in the effort to blame the other for the loss of their shared dream. What they failed to understand was that the dream was never shared. It was, instead, each partner's image of what a marriage should be. It was a mean, nasty, ugly, expensive divorce and it shocked everyone who had once marveled at their "perfect" romance, their "perfect" partnership, their "perfect" marriage.

This is a dramatic example of a couple in Stage 3 whose transitional crisis ended in divorce instead of the counselor's office. But there is more to this story and we will meet Bruce and Nancy again.

First, however, let's revisit Betsy and Link, whose story reveals the

Figure 3: Stage 3: Disintegration

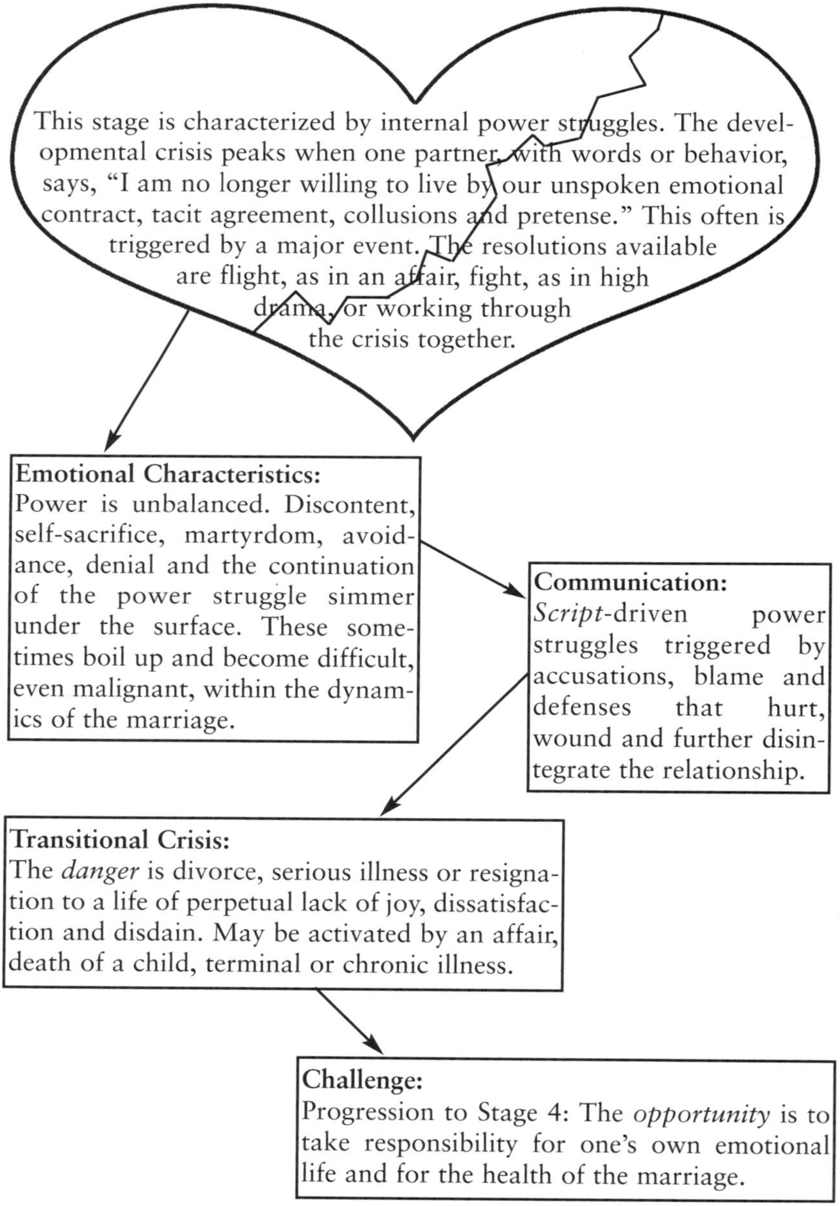

This stage is characterized by internal power struggles. The developmental crisis peaks when one partner, with words or behavior, says, "I am no longer willing to live by our unspoken emotional contract, tacit agreement, collusions and pretense." This often is triggered by a major event. The resolutions available are flight, as in an affair, fight, as in high drama, or working through the crisis together.

Emotional Characteristics:
Power is unbalanced. Discontent, self-sacrifice, martyrdom, avoidance, denial and the continuation of the power struggle simmer under the surface. These sometimes boil up and become difficult, even malignant, within the dynamics of the marriage.

Communication:
Script-driven power struggles triggered by accusations, blame and defenses that hurt, wound and further disintegrate the relationship.

Transitional Crisis:
The *danger* is divorce, serious illness or resignation to a life of perpetual lack of joy, dissatisfaction and disdain. May be activated by an affair, death of a child, terminal or chronic illness.

Challenge:
Progression to Stage 4: The *opportunity* is to take responsibility for one's own emotional life and for the health of the marriage.

extreme tragedy that can result when couples get stuck in the disinte-grative characteristics of Stage 3. This is the married couple we last saw in Stage 2 who fell into an ugly, repetitive pattern of attack, blame and withdrawal fueled by her angry father and his neglectful mother. Even with counseling, this couple did not see the roles their childhood *scripts* and *inner family theaters* played in creating the chaos and pain that dominated their relationship. Nor were they willing to take responsibil-ity for their own emotional lives in the marriage.

They became locked in the simmering hostility of Stage 3 but did not consider divorce. Eventually, Link had an affair and the trap of deceit, hypocrisy, cruelty and abuse that had formed the basis of their childhoods now became their marital way of life. Betsy moved to another state and Link developed heart disease and diabetes. He followed Betsy to her new home, hoping for some help in coping with his illness. Betsy could not bring herself to give him the help he sought and Link died alone. Betsy's unresolved anger left her bitter. She contin-ued to smoke and overeat and suffered a massive heart attack. Six months following Link's demise, Betsy too, was dead. Given the conditions that led to their early deaths, one might conclude that they both died—literally—of broken hearts.

Betsy and Link became locked in one *marital melodrama* that turned into a dance of death. By contrast, David and Shelley are a stel-lar example of a near-disaster turned into a happy transition to Stage 4: Rapprochement.

David and Shelley both come from dysfunctional house-holds where they were forced to grow up too soon. Each took care of younger siblings and assumed other household respon-sibilities, sacrificing normal, care-free childhoods. True to form, Shelley helped David through college and law school. Together, they raised two children, both of whom went on to college. This couple is typical of many in Stage 3 who live for years in a period of settled calm. David and Shelley reared their family and worked as an effective and loving team. When the empty nest presented itself, however, they each began to feel the effects of unrecognized childhood scripts. David longed for the fun and adventure he'd missed as a youth; Shelley needed the security of tradition and belonging that she'd missed in the chaotic home of her childhood. Disappointed by Shelley's inability to provide what he thought he needed, David began an "affair of the mind" with a young paralegal. Shelley sensed his discontent and withdrew, threatening the tradition and security she sought in her marriage.

As we worked together, David came to understand that he was projecting the disappointment and anger he'd felt toward his mother onto Shelley. At the same time, Shelley learned that her own "free child" was shut down in her childhood home—where abuse and high drama ruled. The successful transition to Stage 4 occurred when Shelley created her own sense of tradition, peace and security for herself and David took care of his own emotional need for fun and adventure without turning to either Shelley or a younger woman to fill it for him.

An Important Word about Extramarital Affairs

One affair is a signal of serious malaise in the marriage. It needs to be addressed as an individual issue by the partner who had the affair, by the partner who was betrayed and by the couple whose marriage was impacted by the betrayal. One extramarital affair can induce partners to come together in a more conscious, intimate and forgiving way. If, however, there are multiple affairs, then that is a clue to a character disorder on the part of the partner who has engaged in this behavior, a signal to that partner to take responsibility for his or her own behavior and seek professional help to understand and resolve it. Most marriages do not survive a second affair.

Let's look at Figure 4, Rapprochement.

Mark and Mary were a couple who exhibited all the emotional characteristics of rapprochement. When they married

Figure 4: Stage 4: Rapprochement

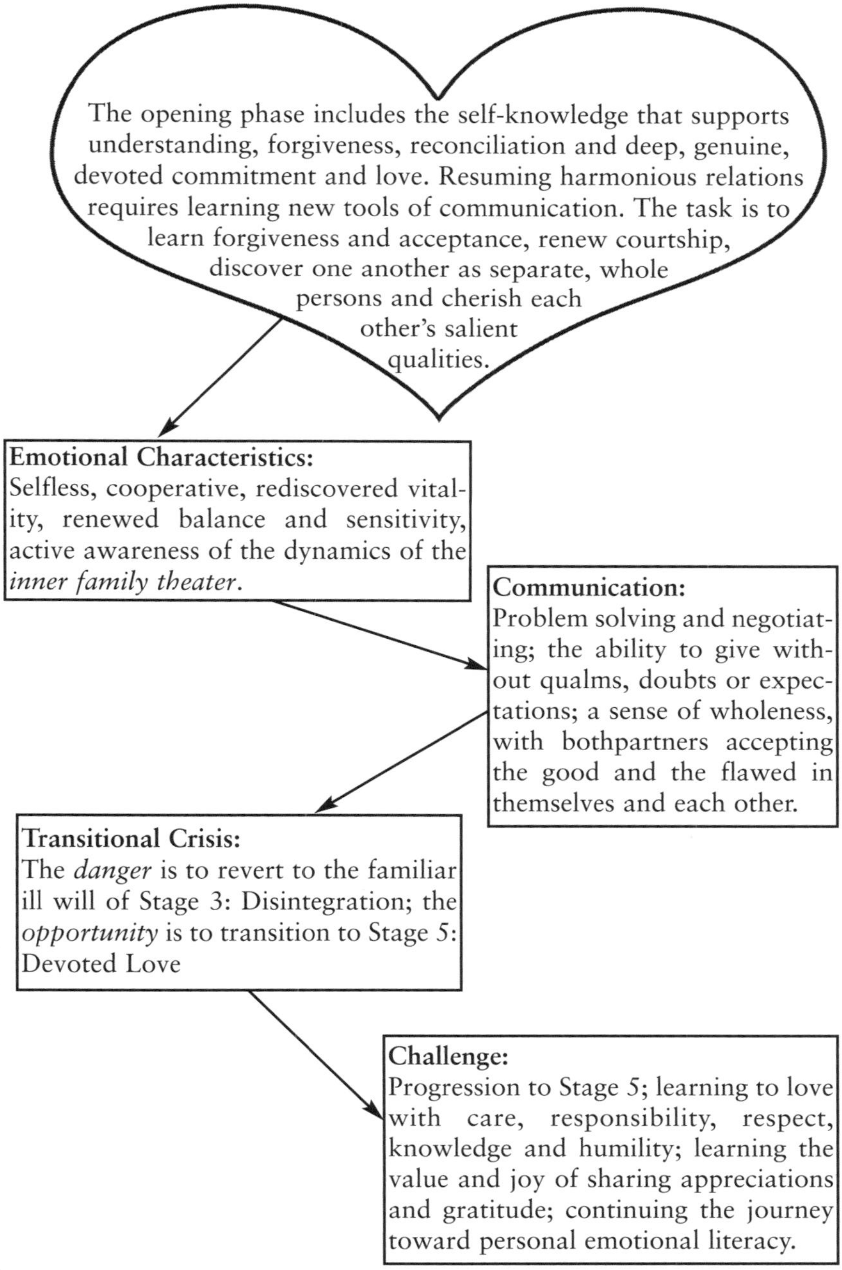

The opening phase includes the self-knowledge that supports understanding, forgiveness, reconciliation and deep, genuine, devoted commitment and love. Resuming harmonious relations requires learning new tools of communication. The task is to learn forgiveness and acceptance, renew courtship, discover one another as separate, whole persons and cherish each other's salient qualities.

Emotional Characteristics:
Selfless, cooperative, rediscovered vitality, renewed balance and sensitivity, active awareness of the dynamics of the *inner family theater*.

Communication:
Problem solving and negotiating; the ability to give without qualms, doubts or expectations; a sense of wholeness, with bothpartners accepting the good and the flawed in themselves and each other.

Transitional Crisis:
The *danger* is to revert to the familiar ill will of Stage 3: Disintegration; the *opportunity* is to transition to Stage 5: Devoted Love

Challenge:
Progression to Stage 5; learning to love with care, responsibility, respect, knowledge and humility; learning the value and joy of sharing appreciations and gratitude; continuing the journey toward personal emotional literacy.

three years ago, they agreed to work hard to blend their families. They have four children between them from previous marriages. They did not enter this marriage blindly or naively; they thought they understood the challenge before them. These two complement one another well, balancing their strengths and weaknesses. They understand that love is a choice you make every day and they are both excellent listeners.

Yet, inevitably, their inner family theaters *began to dominate their relationship. Mary's childhood fostered a feeling of unworthiness, while Mark's created a fear of abandonment. When Mary pushes at Mark to make her feel worthy, the trauma of his childhood is ignited and he withdraws in fear and anger. This in turn exacerbates Mary's feelings of unworthiness and the scenario escalates. They each create the chaos and dynamics that characterized their painful childhoods in the attempt to "fix" it.*

What holds them together? Commitment. They both understand that commitment and forgiveness are key and they are willing to go to any length to get it. With professional guidance, they learned to identify the triggers in each other's words and actions that bring on the marital melodrama. *And they learned that fighting was not the end of the world.*

The meaning of the word commitment became firmly cemented in their lives during one memorable fight. Mark withdrew and became hurt, upset and angry. Mary caught herself before slipping into the unworthy child of her inner family theater *and announced, "It's just a fight, that's all it is. It's not the end of the marriage; you are not being abandoned; it's just a fight." The light came back into Mark's eyes and they both understood the meaning of their commitment to each other. They were able to use the fight as an opportunity to define a problem that needed solving. With new-found awareness of themselves and each other, they were able to move into Stage 5.*

In the midst of their toughest arguments, Mark and Mary did not revert to Stage 3 disintegration or cling to the illusion of Stage 1 romance, but rather used their new communication skills to solve problems, express forgiveness and recommit to their love for each other. They have taken responsibility for their own emotional literacy and have learned to express appreciation and gratitude.

Even hopelessness can give way to love when there is willingness and commitment as you can see in Figure 5.

Another couple with whom I worked had nearly given up on their marriage.

Karen and Jim have been married for fourteen years. They each have grown children from prior marriages and are raising a child of their own. Karen is a pediatric nurse; Jim is a law enforcement retiree who owns and manages an avocado grove and other business ventures. Karen grew up in a neat, clean, upper-middle-class home with three siblings. Her mother was a "two-fisted, Scotch-drinking alcoholic" who did not listen to the needs of her children. As a result, Karen's childhood script tells her it's futile to ask for what she wants. She buried her feelings and hid her anger, pain and disappointment behind a wall of silence. Jim grew up in a messy, working-class home where there was never enough, giving him a poverty mentality. His family never acknowledged birthdays or anniversaries and Jim never learned how. Nor did he understand the value of those things. Conflicting money and household issues also stemmed from their differing childhoods. By the time they came to counseling, Karen had completely lost her "voice" in the marriage and Jim did not know how to listen. Her "heart had turned to stone" (her words), while Jim just went blithely along, not listening, oblivious to Karen's needs.

In the counseling process, they each discovered the inner family origins of their feelings and became willing to change the scripts *that drove them. Karen began to find her voice and was able more and more to articulate her needs; Jim acknowledged the methods he'd used to avoid listening to her and stopped defending his position with sarcasm and teasing. They*

Figure 5: Stage 5: Devoted Love

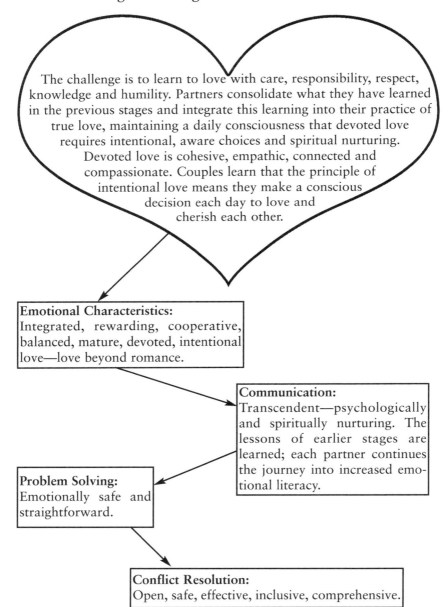

The challenge is to learn to love with care, responsibility, respect, knowledge and humility. Partners consolidate what they have learned in the previous stages and integrate this learning into their practice of true love, maintaining a daily consciousness that devoted love requires intentional, aware choices and spiritual nurturing. Devoted love is cohesive, empathic, connected and compassionate. Couples learn that the principle of intentional love means they make a conscious decision each day to love and cherish each other.

Emotional Characteristics:
Integrated, rewarding, cooperative, balanced, mature, devoted, intentional love—love beyond romance.

Communication:
Transcendent—psychologically and spiritually nurturing. The lessons of earlier stages are learned; each partner continues the journey into increased emotional literacy.

Problem Solving:
Emotionally safe and straightforward.

Conflict Resolution:
Open, safe, effective, inclusive, comprehensive.

each began to see and respect the many outstanding qualities in the other and learned to problem-solve cooperatively, without the scripted dialogue that plagued them in the past. They now work hard at listening, learning and working through the issues one at a time—as they come up—and with the practice of kindness. They are now committed to creating a mature and intentional love between them.

Jim and Karen had decided to separate before they agreed to give counseling a try. Karen's inability to voice her feelings and Jim's inability to intuit them brought them to the transitional crisis of Stage 4. Chronic arguing, loss of respect, buried anger and resentment and a feeling of hopelessness pervaded the relationship. However, instead of reverting to the silent hostility of Stage 3, the futile power struggle of Stage 2 or the damaging illusion of Stage 1, these two became willing to face the pain of their childhoods and learn how that played out in their relationship. They decided to love and accept each other and drop the unrealistic expectation that their marriage should just *work* without the work. The result has been a successful transition to Stage 5 and the development of a truly loving, passionate, devoted and rewarding marriage.

The length of each stage in a couple's journey depends on the *scripts* of the partners, the resilience of the commitment, the willingness of each partner to address the issues between them in emotionally healthy ways, the economic health of the family unit and the physical health of the family members.

The key decision at the time of crisis in each stage is dependent upon the emotional literacy each partner has acquired. Conscious awareness of the dynamics of the *inner family theaters* makes partners less likely to fall prey to the dynamics of their *scripts*.

The two Endeavors that follow this chapter are designed to help you and your partner uncover the origins of your *scripts* so that as a couple you can become more emotionally literate, more fully conscious, more deeply aware of the childhood family dynamics that continue to run your lives. In "Behind the Scenes," you and your partner will uncover the ideas and behaviors you brought from your families into your marriage. In "Setting the Stage," you'll discover the key defenses and decisions that helped you survive your childhoods, but create only distance and discord in your present lives.

Making the decision to create an intentionally loving and devoted partnership means letting go of the illusion of romance and making a commitment to work on the relationship. In the next chapter, we'll see what it is that makes all this worthwhile. What is it that both partners are really after? Are you both willing to do what it takes to achieve this goal?

Endeavor: Behind the Scenes

Overview

To become better acquainted with the origins of your *scripts*, each partner should complete the following questionnaire. The answers will disclose to you the elements of the promptbook for your *marital melodrama*. If you are not able to answer specifically what happened in your childhood, that's okay. Simply write down your first hunch or impression about how you think it was or how you felt it was. Your perception of what went on in your family is more important than what actually happened. After all, you make your decisions in your present relationship largely based on those perceptions.

Activities

Once again, find a quiet place where each partner can read and write brief responses to the next questions in his or her individual notebook. Use your first thoughts and resist the temptation to change them to make the information seem better. If you were raised by people other than your parents, simply substitute their names. Agree upon a time to get back together and share your responses.

My Parents' Marriage and Our Marriage

1. What kind of marriage did your parents have while you were growing up?
2. How did your father show his love to your mother?
3. How did your mother show her love to your father?
4. How do you show love to your partner?
5. What did your father do when he disagreed with your mother?
6. What did your mother do when she disagreed with your father?
7. What do you do when you disagree with your partner?
8. Who made most of the decisions in your parents' marriage?
9. Who makes most of the decisions in your marriage?
10. Was your family religious? What part does religion play in your life today?

11. Was there much sickness in your family? What did your mother and father do when someone became sick?

12. How do you act when your partner or a family member is sick? How does your partner act when you or a family member is sick?

13. When you were a child, who did the chores?

14. Who does the chores now?

15. What did your parents do for fun?

16. What do you and your partner do for fun?

17. Did either of your parents have a favorite motto, saying or phrase? What was it?

18. How do these sayings or mottos affect you today?

19. How did your parents praise and comfort you when you were little?

20. How do you praise and comfort your family now?

21. When things went wrong in your family, what feelings did your mother and father have and show? How did you know?

22. What feelings are you most likely to experience when things go wrong in your present family? How do you express them?

Three Final Questions

1. If you could have changed anything about your parents' marriage when you were young, what would that have been?

2. If you could change anything in your relationship by just wishing, what would it be?

3. Can you find the way or ways in which your early family dynamics provide the elements of the *marital melodrama* in your marriage?

Now you and your partner should get together and share your responses, taking turns. Ask questions that bring clarification and understanding and remember to make no judgmental, teasing or joking comments. Listen carefully through the words to the feelings and the story being told by the other person. See if you can hear any echoes in your relationship today.

Sharing the Process

Answer these questions together. There is no need to write them in your notebooks unless you choose to do it.

- Share two or more examples of the ways in which the dynamics of family life in your childhood have become *triggers* for how you react today.
- Were there any surprises?
- What was helpful to you as you learned about your family dynamics?
- What was helpful to you as you learned about your partner's family dynamics?

Appreciations

Again, remember to use eye contact, listen carefully and don't interrupt.

- Share one or two focused appreciations that flowed from listening to your partner's sharing about his or her family dynamics.

Close With—

- Give your partner a warm embrace and a tender, appreciative "I love you."

Endeavor: Setting the Stage

Overview
In previous Endeavors, we have learned about the players and what happened behind the scenes. Now it will be helpful to know that, as we grew up, we developed a set of tools for survival on the stage of our families of origin. Known as our key defenses, these tools evolved to insure our psychological survival in childhood. As adults, we use these same key defenses for psychological survival in our marriages and in the groups to which we belong. All of these defenses operate from the unconscious level. You and your partner are going to dismantle your dysfunctional key defenses, but not at a rate that will arouse an intolerable level of fear and anxiety.

Activities
Take some time alone to read the definitions of key defenses and then answer the questions that follow in your individual notebooks. Agree on a time to come together and share your responses.

Key Defenses
1. **Denial**
    Painful, anxiety-producing thoughts are screened out. You ignore actions and behaviors of your own that don't fit your beliefs about who you are.
    Two examples:
    *   "I can stop smoking and drinking anytime I choose."
    *   With an angry tone of voice you say, "No! I'm not angry, I'm just fine."
    Identify any denials that you engage in.

2. **Introjection**
    The process of incorporating another person's or group's behaviors, standards or values into your own personality.
    Some examples are:

- My father, who was never on time for anything, by example taught me to do the same.
- My mother disciplined me with a wooden spoon the same way I discipline my children.
- My mother was a really good nurturer and I nurture the same way.
- I dressed and behaved like my high school circle of friends.

Identify some behaviors and values you introjected from your parents or peer groups from your childhood or teenage years.

3. **Projection**
    Unacceptable impulses and thoughts are attributed to others or to your partner; personal failures are blamed on your partner or others.
    Here are two examples:
    - The husband's carelessness with expenses results in a failure to make his business turn a profit. He then criticizes his wife for not watching carefully enough what she is spending of the household money. (He projects onto his wife the carelessness that is unacceptable for him to see in himself.)
    - The wife continually cuts her husband off in the middle of his sentences and then gets angry at him for not letting her express her feelings fully. (It is unacceptable to her that she might be a bad listener, so she projects that quality onto her husband).

    Can you identify any incidents where you have used projection?

4. **Idealization**
    Conscious or unconscious exaggeration of another person's positive attributes and disregard of his/her imperfections or failings; viewing the other person as perfect or nearly perfect and incorporating those positive attributes into your personality. This "protects" you from feeling ambivalence toward the idealized person.
    Can you identify a person from your childhood such as a parent, grandparent, sports hero, historical or political figure, author or

movie star after whom you patterned some or all of your behaviors? Are you able to identify any characteristics in yourself that you adapted from your idealized person? Are you able to see some of that individual's faults today? Are you able to see some of those faults in yourself today?

5. **Regression**
    Reversion to immature behavior when you are threatened with overwhelming external problems or internal conflicts.
    Two examples are:
    - Under stress you just get sleepy and want to crawl under the covers in your bed.
    - Something makes you frustrated and mad, so you yell and stomp around just as you did when you were a kid.

    Do you remember a time when you felt overwhelmed and were tempted to return, or did return, to a childhood method of coping?

6. **Reaction Formation**
    Unacceptable or threatening impulses are denied by going to the opposite extreme.
    Two examples:
    - You felt angry with your mother and, instead of showing those feelings, you denied them and became a good little boy so she wouldn't reject you.
    - You wanted to be a slob, but you denied these urges and became perfect in every way so you wouldn't get scolded and instead got parental approval.

    How did you run away from your angry, afraid, impulsive feelings? How do you do that today?

7. **Sublimation**
    Channeling unacceptable sexual or aggressive drives into acceptable expression.

Two examples:

- When sexual urges threaten to interfere with a relationship, you may choose to use artistic endeavors as a safe way of expression.
- When feeling angry with your partner, you may use sports as a way of expending that energy.

What have you substituted for unacceptable sexual or aggressive drives?

8. **Intellectualization**

   Emotional problems are dealt with in the abstract or by excessive intellectual activity.

   Two examples:

   - Compulsively reading about or researching a problem to avoid the feelings associated with it.
   - Loving someone in the abstract, not in person; loving the idea of someone.

   Do you ever over-analyze a painful situation in order to avoid feeling the actual emotion? Have you ever been more comfortable with loving the idea of someone, rather than loving that individual as a person?

9. **Rationalization**

   Questionable reasons are given to justify unacceptable behavior or personal shortcomings. This is used to ward off guilt, maintain self-respect and protect yourself from criticism.

   Three examples:

   - "Doesn't everybody cheat on taxes?"
   - "An expensive car saves money in the end."
   - "You have to spank children to toughen them up."

   Have you ever found yourself explaining your behavior to your partner? Do you attack and blame your partner while defending yourself to get your partner to see your point of view?

Now come together as arranged and share your responses to the key defenses of your *scripts*. Remember to take turns and use your Guidelines for Safe Communication.

Sharing the Process
Taking turns, respond to these questions:
- Did you learn anything surprising about yourself?
- Did you learn anything surprising about your partner?
- What was helpful to you as you learned about your personal defenses?
- What was helpful to you as you learned about your partner's defenses?
- Any other thoughts you want to share with each other about what you learned?

Appreciations
Partners should use eye contact, listen carefully and not interrupt each other.
- Share one or two focused appreciations of your partner.
- Share one way in which your partner's sharing was important to you. Be specific; be kind.

Close With—
- Give each other a hug and a genuine "I love you."

A Final Activity
Go out on a date when you complete this endeavor. Celebrate the openness and honesty which now exist between you and how much you have learned about yourselves and your marriage.

PART II:
THE CONSCIOUS RELATIONSHIP

Chapter 5

Welcoming Marriage's Embrace

*The meeting of two personalities is like the
contact of two chemical substances: if there is
any reaction, both are transformed.*
                                        C. G. Jung

What do we really want from love relationships? For those lucky enough to have had safe and good childhoods, perhaps what we want out of marriage or partnership is to recreate what was, to share with our own spouses and children the stable relationships we were given. Some of us are looking for safe havens, places where we can create something different from what we knew as children. Some of us are looking for financial security, a certain kind of lifestyle or simply someone with whom to have fun. And some of us just don't know; we dive into relationships because they feel good at the moment, without much conscious intention or thought. The reasons for coupling up are infinite, but in the end, we all share one objective—we want to be happy. We believe that partners will either make us happy or enhance our existing happiness.

A good marriage is good for you, say the statistics. People who are happily married have fewer health problems and live longer. With the aid of regular affection, closeness and mutual support, people are more productive, more creative, more relaxed. The possibilities in a safe and loving relationship are limitless.

Marriage provides opportunities for intimacy, joy, closeness, nurturing and children. Marriage offers the challenge of creating an institution well anchored in the community that will sustain the partners and the children. Marriage contributes to our personal health and to the health of our children and in so doing ensures the health of community, society, nation and world. To say that marriage and family are the cornerstones of civilization is not just some hackneyed cliché.

For both personal as well as societal—yes, even global—reasons, we need to create, nurture and maintain the institution of marriage. In order to do this, we must prepare for and develop the tools to sustain our primary relationships. Commitment, not romance, will sustain what we have created. What is our mantra? **The only relationship that works is one on which we work.**

The challenge is to get from the illusion of romance to the embrace of marriage in a way that creates a foundation from which healthy relationships can emerge and grow. Long lasting love requires different tools from the ones romance requires. One is magic, illusory; the other is intentional, a choice you must make every day.

However, to arrive at this choice, couples must start with a good dose of reality. Marriage is not a plateau of understanding that, once reached, leaves us nowhere else to go. A good marriage is not the ending of a story, as in… *and they lived happily ever after.* A good marriage is the start of another story, one that begins after the romantic prologue. A good marriage keeps growing, evolving, struggling, transcending. In the words of Sam Keen, who wrote *Fire in the Belly:*

> *Marriage is: an aphrodisiac for the mature; a great yoga; a discipline of incarnate love; a task that stretches a man and a woman to the fullest; a drama in which a man and a woman must gradually divest themselves of their archetypes and*

stereotypes and come to love each other as perfectly flawed human beings.

What an appealing idea! To be loved as flawed human beings, accepted and cherished as much for our faults as for our strengths. And so the vast majority of society continues to court and mate, to seek the warm embrace of marriage—despite the naysayers, despite the fact that some view courtship and marriage as hopelessly archaic, inconvenient, unnecessary and old-fashioned. Courtship and marriage continue to be chosen—sometimes consciously, more often blindly.

As we have seen in part one, when two people come together, each with a unique history, they create together a dynamic that is distinctive. This distinctiveness is felt to be magical or some kind of chemistry. The reality is that relationships, in courtship and in marriage, are between real men and real women, not mythical or idealized partners. Authentic men and women come together and create between them the joy of two lives well-lived. Despite games, codes and stratagems, men and women still manage to create the cohesion and the trust needed to be together.

When we accept that happiness is created, that its achievement is not magic, we can make conscious, intentional choices—and step into the embrace of a lasting marriage or partnership. At this point in our work together we have released certain fundamental beliefs about romantic love, such as the one that says there is only one right person, a soulmate, for us. We have released our belief in being certain or in the idea that when it's right, we'll just know. Finally, we have released the belief that marriage is an end and have learned that it is an ever-evolving continuation.

Change is inevitable in marriage. Partners, circumstances and health change; ideas, communities and society change. A dynamic and evolving marriage can meet dynamic and changing times. Change brings challenge and richness to marriage. Partners in a committed marriage will respond to the stresses of change as stimulation and inspiration to learn more about themselves and each other.

All marriages go through periods of disillusionment, disappointment, frustration and even hopelessness. When those feelings are addressed in constructive ways, when both partners agree that the marriage is worth working on and agree to get help, the partnership grows and evolves as it should. Negative feelings are connected to positive, warm and intimate feelings that people expect from marriage. They are necessary to each other and cannot exist separately.

When we understand and accept that relationships are created intentionally, it is possible to posit a *Law of Family Well-Being*. That law states: *The life of an effective family depends upon successfully processing the ongoing emotional life within it*. When followed, it is our first step into the warm embrace of marriage and to emotionally healthy partnering.

Our next step is to identify the five essential ingredients of a healthy, rewarding and nurturing relationship. These are *friendship, compatibility, affection, commitment* and *sensuality*. Cultivating these five essential ingredients requires that we pay attention, that we develop—consciously and intentionally—the relationship we seek. In chapter 9: Developing Harmony Together, we'll be looking in more detail at these essential five elements.

The cohesive force that holds these elements together and supports the vitality of a relationship is love. Love enables us to meet the challenges and survive the threats, both internal and external, to our partnerships. Love encompasses a wide range of emotions, feelings and acts—deeply rooted in heart, mind and soul—that form the foundation for a committed relationship. It is caring, kindness, thoughtfulness and, most of all, forgiveness—asked when needed and given when felt. Love is sustained through thick and thin, through illness and adversity, through joy and sorrow. The harvest is tenderness, compassion, joyfulness and empathy.

The expression of that love is possible only when two persons communicate with each other from the center of their existence. Erich Fromm wrote in *The Art of Love*:

> *The ability to love depends upon one's capacity to emerge from narcissism, and from the incestuous fixation to mother and clan; it depends upon our capacity to grow, to develop a*

productive orientation in our relationship toward the world and ourselves. This process of emergence, of birth, of waking up, requires one quality as a necessary condition: faith.

Free of control, domination, expectations and demands, this faith is not submissive. Rather, it is autonomous and productive. Faith in ourselves, in our partners and in the value of a committed relationship is a fundamental requirement as partners journey together into the warm embrace of intentional love.

When all is said and done, we must agree that it's worth it. If you and your partner are reading this book, you have likely come to that conclusion. For those of us who have traveled this road, who have taken the risks and done the work, the resounding and unanimous conclusion is yes, it's worth it!

A vital marriage is a work of art created by the partners that brings zest, replenishment, creativity and meaning to their own and each other's lives. A vital, loving relationship allows us to enjoy the full spectrum of human emotions, to laugh all the laughter and to weep all the tears. The warm embrace of marriage invites us to experience fully who we are in an emotionally safe and restorative place. When we are free to be who we really are, the expression of that will, in turn, enrich the marriage, bring the relationship to life and foster full and rewarding intimacy.

In the Endeavor that follows this chapter, you will express full acceptance and appreciation of one another. You will establish your own unique methods and rituals for keeping your relationship vital, intriguing, fun and, yes, romantic—as well as caring and supportive. It will be a welcome relief from the difficult work of the previous Endeavors, but no less important!

When you welcome the warm embrace of intentional love, you acknowledge the hope that you can get what you want in a relationship. In chapter 6, you will learn that in order to achieve this, you must also have faith in the relationship, that it—as an entity separate from yourselves—deserves the same love and attention you give to one another. With the acknowledgment of all three, you and your partner can co-create the happy life you want.

Endeavor: Courting, Sharing and Caring

Overview

The goal of this Endeavor is to spice up your relationship. When your relationship seems humdrum, boring, careworn, overburdened or routine, these activities will bring intentional sharing, caring and courtship back into your lives. To carry out the daily activities of life—what Robert A. Johnson, author of *We: Understanding the Psychology of Romantic Love*, calls "stirring oatmeal"—is a privilege that requires your nurturing and gratitude. When "stirring oatmeal" seems boring, you must learn to celebrate the stability, joy, love and care that such daily life symbolizes.

That romance sometimes seems absent may be a blessing, for in its absence, you can truly experience your partner fully and completely. Once you understand that love is a choice you make every day, then you can enliven it with both devotion and excitement.

The following activities may seem strained and artificial at first, but the goal is to make them habitual and easy. They are designed to lead you into thoughtful connections with your partner. It's also important to remember anniversaries, holidays, birthdays, special times. Celebrate these with cards, flowers or other thoughtful ways.

Once you have experimented with the activities suggested here, you can design your own creative ways to celebrate each other that are uniquely suited to you and your partner as individuals and to your style as a couple.

Activities

1. Sharing Times

At the end of the working day, give each other a hug and take ten minutes to share your day with each other. If you have children or extended family members living in the household or visiting, include them in this activity. Each person shares, one by one. Do not interrupt the person speaking, except to call time if one is taking more than his or her fair share of time (it may be necessary to do this with children). Do this activity daily until it becomes a family habit.

2. **Caring Acts**
   - Give your partner one unsolicited caring act a day.
   - Ask your partner for one caring act a day.

   (Yes, these are separate. You will give the one that is unsolicited and you will also give the one that is requested, for a total of two.)

3. **Courtship Events**

   Take turns arranging a date with your partner each week (one partner the first week, the other the next). Be thoughtful and caring in your choices, keeping in mind what your partner likes and appreciates. It can be as simple as a walk in a favorite spot or as extravagant as a romantic getaway weekend. Or something in-between, like a meal at a favorite restaurant, a visit to a local art gallery or attending a musical event. Arrange for the childcare and other household needs. The key element here is each partner should take complete responsibility for the date, from the asking to the arranging to the end—freeing the other to enjoy it fully.

4. **Unexpected and Random Acts of Thoughtfulness**

   Affirming your partner repeatedly is crucial to your relationship. There is no such thing as too much or too often. Acknowledge and celebrate your partner's inner and outer beauty, specialness, talents and absolute *OKness*. Handmade or specially chosen cards, pictures and notes are a wonderful way to do this. Send messages that say "I believe in you," "I'm so proud of you," "I have faith in you," "You are wonderful because…," "You are wonderful *just* because." Discover the small, precious ways that your partner likes to be told he or she is loved, cherished, appreciated by you. Incorporate them often into your daily lives together. Notes in a lunch box, messages on a voice mail, endearing or encouraging E-mails. Notes left at home to greet your partner while you are out, flowers, a pot of homemade soup or favorite dish, a fresh loaf of bakery bread, a new music CD from a favorite artist—all of these things and more are ways to cherish, honor and remind the one you love that you're glad he or she is your partner. This will become a life-long habit—one that feels as good to give as to receive.

Sharing the Process

Do these activities for a month. In your notebooks, jot down the date a month from now with a reminder to write a few thoughts about how these get-togethers have affected your relationship. Include your answers to the following questions in your individual notebooks.

- How is the Sharing Times activity going?
- Are you keeping up with your Caring Acts?
- Have you followed through on the Courtship Events?
- Are there changes or improvements to these activities that would better fit your situation?
- Have you committed any unexpected and random acts of kindness lately?

Now get together and share your responses, taking turns and using your Guidelines for Safe Communication.

Appreciations

- Give your partner two appreciations focused on his/her participation in these partnership renewal activities.
- Share one or two ways you were affected by each of the exercises.

Close With—

- A warm embrace and an "I love you."

Chapter 6

Recognizing Me,
You and the Relationship

We do not see things as they are, but as we are.
The Talmud

In every marriage there are not two but three entities, each requiring equal attention, nourishment and love. Every long lasting partnership must allow time and room for *you, me* and *us*. It is as important to maintain the *us* in good health through daily, thoughtful, conscious devotion as it is the *you* and the *me*. Recognizing that there is a third life in your marriage, the relationship itself, is crucial. In this chapter, you will spend some time learning to recognize, include and attend to this third entity.

Let's examine what happens to the relationship as it progresses through the five stages of couple development.

Stage 1: Romance

In this illusory stage, the couple believes that love will conquer all. The communication goal is to sustain that illusion and to entrust the other with the impossible task of filling unmet childhood needs. The crisis comes when the illusion of romance is shattered by reality. The challenge for each partner is to become aware of the differences between themselves.

In chapter 1 we discussed Peter and Rebecca, the former workmates who fell madly in love twenty years after their first meeting, only to break up when the reality that they had fallen in love with illusions set in. Although each time they reconciled Rebecca said she would change what he didn't like and Peter promised he would point out these things, he didn't, feeling that he "shouldn't have to teach her how to treat him." Peter needed respect, attention and kindness and he wanted them expressed in certain ways. Yet he refused to ask for those things, expecting Rebecca to intuit his needs. Rebecca needed honesty, sharing and caring. Yet in her desperate longing for the romance that began their courtship, she submerged her needs and expected love to conquer all.

How could their acknowledgment of and attention to the third entity—the relationship—have changed their approach and the outcome? Had these two paid the same conscious, devoted attention to the relationship as they did to their own needs, my long experience counseling couples has shown, they *might* have been able to see beyond the illusion of romance to the real value they brought to each other. If Rebecca had included and attended to the relationship, not just to her desire to have one, Peter might not have felt neglected or dismissed in the first place. If Peter had placed their relationship as equal in importance to his needs, he might not have abandoned it.

Stage 2: The Politics of Love

In this stage, the illusion of romance has been shattered, causing conflict and imbalance. Many couples struggle and become delayed or frozen at this point when communication is dominated by *script*-driven power struggles. The crisis comes when one or both partners withdraws or capitulates. The challenge is for each partner to take responsibility for his or her feelings and behaviors.

The two most common reasons for the crisis of this stage are enmeshment and hostile-dependence. Enmeshment occurs when one partner surrenders to the dominance of the other and swallows all contrary or problematic feelings. The couple soon looks, acts, believes and often dresses alike. The partner who surrenders may somaticize (take on the bodily manifestations of) his or her feelings, anxieties and stresses, developing real and/or imaginary pain and illness.

Hostile-dependence occurs when a couple sinks into a pattern of antagonism followed by some form of tolerable dependence while awaiting an opportunity to renew the hostilities. Some couples maintain this negative positioning throughout their marriages. Hostile-dependence characteristics include unspoken expectations, habitual argumentative behavior, denial and defensive responses, as well as aggressive and passive-aggressive behaviors. Explosiveness and abuse may be frequent in a marriage experiencing this situation. Nagging and resentments are ever present and the *inner family theater* dominates. The internal power struggles are pervasive.

The *us* entity commonly manifests itself around how chores and money are to be thought about, shared and managed. Remember from chapter 2 how Gwen, the conscientious, workaholic nurse and her partner Lance, the hypersensitive entrepreneur, who fell in love at first sight enacted a *family theater* that placed her alcoholic father and his critical, punishing mother at center stage. Their power struggles began quite innocently with chores, turned to money issues and often ended with slamming doors. The outcome might have been different if their marriage had been given equal time and attention.

Stage 3: Disintegration

One or both partners back out of the unspoken emotional contract made in Stage 2, demonstrating by their behavior that they are no longer willing to live the way they were. Communication is still restricted to the *script*-driven power struggle. Self-driven and unbalanced emotion leads to a crisis such as divorce or serious illness. If you recognize your relationship is at this stage, the challenge is to translate feelings which stem from the pain of past experiences into emotions that fit the present.

Another couple, Georgia and Tom, never did find the *we* in their relationship. Their twenty-year partnership was plagued by the effects of Georgia, the child of an alcoholic father, being "parentized" by age eight and Tom being the child of a successful but demanding father who had pushed him into a career he didn't want. Tom eventually abandoned this career to become a struggling artist, which forced Georgia into becoming not only the main wage earner, but the chief caretaker of their four children.

Despite Georgia's repeated pleading to get help, this couple never recognized or understood the actors in their *inner family theaters* nor the *scripts* that drove them. Georgia projected onto Tom the rage she felt toward her father, leaving little room for negotiation or compromise. Tom remained mired in the paralysis he felt at his failure to be successful in either of his careers. This turned into shame and then resentment, until finally they divorced. How would that realization that there was a third party to be recognized—the marriage—have changed their feelings and in turn, altered their behavior?

One couple whom we discussed did attain that realization. Bruce and Nancy's once "perfect" marriage disintegrated through unrealistic expectations and ended in a nasty divorce. Four years after the divorce became final, this couple did what Georgia and Tom never did—recognized the importance of *us*.

> *In the aftermath of their painful divorce, both Bruce and Nancy sought help. Individually and then together in the counselor's office and support group, they gained enough insight to acknowledge their own responsibility for their demise as a couple. Bruce also acknowledged his alcohol problem and became devoted to his sobriety. In the process of making amends to Nancy, their love was reignited. They began to date and became willing to work hard at knowing themselves better, learning to communicate more effectively and practicing forgiveness. It became clear to them that in any relationship, there is a "me," a "you" and an "us"—each one to be nurtured and respected.*

Stage 4: Rapprochement

In this stage all the work couples have done pays off. Partners become selfless, cooperative, sensitive and balanced. Communication involves problem-solving and negotiation, giving without doubt or expectation. A crisis can occur if the couple allows fear of losing what they have to throw them back into the illusion of romance. The challenge is to share appreciation and express gratitude. Mark and Mary, one of the couples we met in chapter 4, created a blended family of four children successfully. When childhood *scripts* (Mark's fear of abandonment and Mary's feelings of unworthiness) threatened their marriage, their strong commitment brought understanding.

> *Mary: "Damn it, Mark! It was important to me that we show up for this dinner. I really wanted to be a part of this. I thought you did, too."*
>
> *Mark: "I did, Mary! I just forgot that it was this weekend."*
>
> *Mary: "How could you just forget? I must have reminded you ten times last week. Sometimes I just don't know where your priorities are!"*
>
> *Mark: "Look, Mary, I'm sorry we missed the dinner; I know it was important to you. It was important to me, too, and you can believe that or not."*
>
> *Mary: "Now, don't go putting this back on me, Mark. It's not about believing you; it's about suiting up and showing up for the things in life that are important."*
>
> *Mark: [walking out of the room] "Mary, I don't know what you want me to do, but we can't go on arguing like this."*
>
> *Mary: [following him into the next room and standing directly in front of him, eye to eye] "Whoa, Mark. This is just a fight, that's all it is. It's not the end of the marriage! You are not being abandoned; you're not even being threatened. It's just a fight. That's all."*

Mark: [after a long silence, a smile of recognition replaces the frown of Mark's face] "I'm running scared again, aren't I? Ok, hon. Let's see where we go from here."

As soon as Mary recognized that her words had triggered Mark's Not OK Child, she placed the relationship ahead of her own needs and created an opportunity for a new awareness. In this scene, she also stopped herself from slipping into her own unworthy child so she could be fully present for the relationship. They were then able to use the fight to solve a problem that needed a solution. How might it have gone differently if they had not protected the marriage as a separate entity, but limited their feelings only to themselves and each other?

Stage 5: Devoted Love

In this stage emotions are integrated, cooperative and balanced. Communication between partners is transcendent and psychologically and spiritually nurturing.

Karen and Jim, the couple from chapter 4, transcended their childhood *scripts* and created a marriage flourishing in Stage 5. This is the couple in which Karen lost her voice and Jim couldn't hear. Counseling and commitment taught Karen it was safe to ask for what she wanted and needed and taught Jim to discard his habit of teasing in favor of empathic and caring listening. How is the life of the marriage acknowledged by these two? What would be different if it were not a vital part of this couple's awareness?

As you learn to think of the relationship as worthy of care and attention, you will also learn to cherish everyday, ordinary togetherness instead of attempting to sustain the illusion of romance. Robert A. Johnson aptly describes this:

Stirring oatmeal is a humble act—not exciting or thrilling. But it symbolizes a relatedness that brings human beings down to earth. It represents a willingness to share ordinary human life, to find meaning in the simple, unromantic tasks: earning a living, living within a budget, putting out the garbage, feed-

ing the baby in the middle of the night. To "stir oatmeal"
means to find the relatedness, the value, even beauty, in simple
ordinary things, not to eternally demand a cosmic drama, an
entertainment, or an extraordinary intensity in everything.

There is something intensely comforting about the things a couple share during the Devoted Love stage of their development. It doesn't much matter what they are doing. The comfort comes from their feeling love as they go about the everyday tasks of their lives.

It is important to understand the joy and find the *magic* in the ordinariness of a loving couple. We only need be deprived of this to realize how valuable it is. In the Endeavor that follows, "One Together, Two Together," you will make some surprising discoveries about the time you spend together. You will learn to respect and value your individual need for time alone and reveal to each other the secret joys of "stirring oatmeal" with your partner, this one-of-a-kind person.

Endeavor: One Together, Two Together

Overview
The goal of this Endeavor is to raise your awareness about each other's separate needs and the joint needs of your relationship. Chapter 6 teaches that a marriage or partnership is about *you*, *me* and *us*. Each must be cultivated and nurtured. It is a romantic illusion that "if my partner does not want to be with me all the time or does not know at all times what I am thinking, what I am feeling and what I want, my partner must not love me." The following activities will demonstrate this illusion and help you become better acquainted with the rhythms that give you time apart and then bring you back together.

Activities
Write your responses to the following tasks in your individual note-books.

1. **Time Together**
   • Create a list of things you truly enjoy doing together.

2. **Time Alone**
   • What would you most like to accomplish or do by yourself that you are not now doing?
   • Write how and when you might like to accomplish each one.

Now come together and share your responses to Activities 1 and 2 with each other. As you listen to your partner, think about the ways in which you can support your partner in the effort to accomplish items from his or her list. Jot your ideas down and share them.

3. **What I Want from You**
Write down three acts of caring that you are not now receiving from your partner for which you secretly long. Include the when and how wherever possible. Be specific, not vague. For example: "I want you to appreciate me more" is too vague; "I want you to tell me when you

especially like what I have cooked for dinner" is better. "I wish you'd spend more time with me" is too vague; "I would like you to join me for a half-hour walk in the evenings" is better. "I want you to be more tender with me" is too vague; "I'd love to have you stroke my hair when we're finished making love and starting to fall asleep," is much better.

Now come together, share your three desires and then identify for each other the ones you are willing to give or do now. Identify the ones that are difficult for you to do. Are you willing to work on doing them? How? Be specific, be concrete and be genuine.

Sharing the Process
Take turns and dialogue the following—
- What was the most difficult part of this Endeavor?
- What was the most enjoyable part of this Endeavor?
- Did you discover anything new about yourself or your partner? If so, what was it?

Appreciations
- Share a focused appreciation about your partner's participation.
- Share an appreciation about your partner that recognizes his or her specialness.
- Share an appreciation that you have about the "us" part of your marriage.

Close With—
- A hug and an authentic "I love you."

Chapter 7

The Marital Melodrama—
the Script, the Players,
the Supporting Cast

The first duty of love is to listen.
Paul Tillich

Honest communication in a coupled relationship means a better, happier marriage or partnership. However, how many of us really know how to communicate honestly? How many instead continue, often unaware, to let the characters of our *inner family theaters* run the show? Words, voice inflections, gestures, facial expressions, eye movement and body language may all be used to express the *scripts* of childhood instead of the true self's reactions and feelings. In this chapter, we'll take a closer look at the *marital melodrama*—the conflict that occurs when two *inner family theaters* vie for top billing.

Episodes of the *marital melodrama* generally occur in the second stage of a relationship. Driven by deeply hidden childhood fears, anger, sadness, embarrassment and shame, the melodrama takes over all the emotional channels—anger, joy, fear and sorrow—available to the partners.

The Players

As we discussed in chapter 2, each of the two starring actors in the *marital melodrama* comes with his or her own set of distinct characteristics: the partner who fears he can't be himself, which Joan Lachkar termed *fear of engulfment*; and the partner who fears she will be left alone, which Lachkar called *fear of abandonment*. In discussing further these two kinds of partners, we will be painting a picture that contains most of their worst characteristics. It will be important to remember that the portraits to follow represent the pure extremes of each type. Most of us fall into one of these two categories, but to varying degrees.

For purposes of clarity, throughout this chapter I will refer to the partner who fears engulfment as male and the partner who fears abandonment as female. However, it is important to remember that men are just as likely to fear abandonment and women are just as likely to fear engulfment.

Fear of engulfment is the fear on the part of one partner that he'll lose himself to the domination of the other. He feels special, then insulted or outraged when that specialness is not recognized and acknowledged. He feels afraid that his partner will take away or somehow defeat his freedom.

Fear of abandonment is the fear on the part of the other partner that she will be abandoned. She is needy; she feels she is unworthy of love and so is willing to do anything for her partner in order to feel connected and avoid the terror of emptiness and abandonment.

The partner who fears engulfment is engrossed with self, dominated by thoughts and fantasies that center on entitlement and has an excessive need to prove his specialness. He is preoccupied, even obsessed, with perfectionism; guilt-ridden, he engages in self-persecution, self-rejection and self-hate. He disowns these characteristics, however, and often, through the operation of projection, attacks his partner with persecution, rejection and hatred. He feels he can only be loved through admiration.

The partner who fears abandonment feels she is unlovable. An early unmet need for bonding now causes her to suffer from feelings of emptiness and deprivation. Longing for an all-nurturing mother or father, she will do anything in order to feel some semblance of relatedness. She often has a diminished sense of self and does not feel entitled or deserving. Paradoxically, she is keenly tuned to any failures in her partner and when he does not respect or honor her feelings, she gives way to anger and rage. She is dominated by persecutory anxiety, lack of impulse control and defenses rooted in shame and blame. She is on a constant search to find out who she is and, when threatened, lashes out with retaliatory responses, self-deprecation and, in extreme cases, even self-mutilation.

The *Script*

The two players bring the *scripts* they learned from the *inner family theaters* of their childhoods into their marriage. They maneuver through a sad series of encounters that escalate until one withdraws in hurt and anger. These encounters, which sometimes become abusive, tend to follow a pattern: The partner who fears abandonment needs bonding and attachment in order to feel worthy. She will often re-enact the painful experiences of her past, remaining loyal to the pain of her childhood. The partner who fears engulfment uses withdrawal as punishment, which in turn evokes unconscious anxiety in her. This *script*-driven, repetitive *marital melodrama* involves an interlocking system of needs, pain, rage and self-sacrifice.

Let's go back to Gwen and Lance, whom we first met in chapter 2 and discussed in several chapters. They fell in love at first sight. Gwen, the workaholic nurse, you will recall, had an alcoholic father and a childhood *script* that drove her to be harsh and critical. Lance, the successful entrepreneur, had a punishing mother and a childhood *script* that drove him to be hypersensitive. Following is a scenario from their past that illustrates the repetitive, cyclical, interdependent nature of a *marital melodrama*, wherein their historic fears of engulfment and abandonment control the stage.

> Gwen: "Darn it, Lance. I know it seems like a really small thing, but you left the empty toilet paper roll on the windowsill in the bathroom yesterday. Why couldn't you have put it in the waste basket? Why would you leave it for me to do?"

Lance: "The waste basket wasn't there, Gwen! What did you expect me to do? Run naked through the house to fetch the basket—which, by the way, you left downstairs when you emptied it."

Gwen: "Maybe not right then, OK. But how hard is it to remember and do it after you got dressed? You just don't seem to get how hard I work to keep our home clean and beautiful. That dumb little thing really set me off… it just made me feel like you don't notice or care that I take pride in our home— like you just take me for granted."

Lance: "Oh for god's sake, Gwen. It's just a toilet paper roll. What… now I don't have the right to my own privacy? Now I have to jump through hoops, naked, just to make sure I don't offend you? My habits aren't important? Oh, forget it. This is too ridiculous to even be talking about. I've gotta go to work."

That evening—

Lance: "Gwen, I can't find the rubbing alcohol! I've got a shaving cut that won't stop bleeding. Seen it?"

Gwen: "Oh, I'm sorry. I took it downstairs the other day to clean the printer and forgot to put it back."

Lance: "Yeah, OK. But would you bring it up here please? Looks like I'm not the only one who forgets to put things back where they belong."

Gwen: "Yup. You're right. I hate it when you reach for something and it's not there. I'm sorry, hon."

Lance: "Well OK. But it wouldn't have taken much to remember that I use that stuff more than you do. I wish you'd been a bit more considerate."

We can almost hear the fear of abandonment in Gwen's expressions of need to be appreciated, her nearly desperate search for the respect and honor she missed in her childhood. And we can see classic fear of engulfment in Lance's need to be regarded as special, in his withdrawal from the conversation and then in his *tit for tat* criticism of Gwen's behavior.

The repetitive *marital melodrama* is such a source of conflict for many couples that it will be helpful to look in on a second couple whose interlocking *scripts* keeps them in a cycle of frustration and hurt. Jim and Karen, the couple in their middle years, we've also met earlier. Karen, you will remember, has a *script* that caused her to lose her voice, while Jim's *script* caused him to tease instead of listen. Let's eavesdrop on a conversation that was typical of their marriage before our work on their relationship began.

> Jim: *"Hey, Karen, where'd this new print come from?"*
> Karen: *"I found it at that new art store and thought it would be perfect for the stairwell. Do you like it?"*
> Jim: *"It's OK. But Karen, can we really afford to be buying things like that right now?"*
> Karen: *"Oh, I see. I go out and make the money that keeps this house together, while you stay home and do nothing, except complain about the way I spend it."*
> Jim: *"Come on, honey. I'm not complaining; I just don't think our house needs to look like the Getty."*
> Karen: *"Damn it, Jim, you're avoiding the issue. I am so sick and tired of coming home from a long day at the hospital to find you haven't even loaded the dishwasher or picked up the house or taken out the trash. And I can do without your sarcastic remarks whenever I buy something new."*
> Jim: *"And I can live without your constant nagging about the house. Do you know how much it takes to be here for Bailey during the day, while you're out playing Florence Nightingale?"*
> Karen: *"Thanks very much for respecting my work, Jim. And as for Bailey, sometimes I think you're actually trying to be both mother and father to him. I wish you'd let me be his mother once in awhile."*
> Jim: *"For Pete's sake Karen, now you've really lost it. I'm going to watch the news..."* [Jim leaves the room.]

Jim is exhibiting several qualities of a person fearful of engulfment. The sense of entitlement in his pronouncement about the print being too expensive is decisive. His need to be recognized as special may be seen in his statement about being there for Bailey. Jim is defensive about Karen's demands that he help with the house; he wants to be loved and appreciated for what he does, yet he is guilt-ridden for not doing enough. And he is scared to death he'll lose the very thing he wants most—nurturing from Karen.

In Karen's lack of impulse control (her purchase of a print they can't afford), we see the qualities of a woman afraid of abandonment. She is dominated by defenses rooted in shame as seen in her retort to Jim's query about the print. When feeling threatened, she lashes out at Jim with retaliatory responses such as "I can do without your sarcastic remarks…" and bringing up the issue of housework. Karen is tuned in to Jim's failures and has no problem expressing her anger when she perceives he has not honored her feelings. Her diminished sense of self comes out in her plea to "…let me be [Bailey's] mother once in awhile."

Neither Jim nor Karen recognized that their words, their feelings and their behavior toward each other were governed by fear of engulfment/fear of abandonment issues. While this scene did not escalate into an abusive encounter, Jim did end up withdrawing in hurt and anger. Both partners' tendency to project anger, to blame and to defend kept them and the relationship in an impoverished state.

When life partners are locked into this pattern, they experience a cycle of hope, disappointment and rage. Sig Heilbreich, Holocaust survivor, was asked once how he survived five concentration camps during the Nazi rule in Germany. "Hope begins only when you become aware of your predicament," he replied. Likewise in a *marital melodrama* hope begins only when the two people become aware of their predicament.

The first step toward awareness is to examine internal emotional geography. This book offers a guide to doing just that; a good couples' therapist can also create a safe place to explore that inner emotional geography.

When couples are involved in partnerships mired in negativity like Lance and Gwen's or Jim and Karen's, the very things that bind them together also perpetuate and feed the conflicts between them. One attacks and the other withdraws. The withdrawal awakens the terror of being abandoned and one promises the other the world. Seduced and ever hopeful, the other partner returns and is drawn back into the action by these seemingly well-intentioned promises.

The partner who fears engulfment feels disappointed with the outside world. He has a pervasive sense of guilt and feels a need for a refuge within the relationship where guilt can be assuaged and so he stays. He struggles to do things that will garner the approval and admiration of his partner. The one who fears abandonment remains, because the pain of living with the other is preferred over the terror of living alone.

So far, we have dealt only with couples where one partner fears engulfment and the other fears abandonment. Sometimes, though not often, both partners may fear engulfment or both may fear abandonment. In the first case, these partnerships—without work—sink into a hostile-dependent state that lasts the duration of the marriage. In the second case—if they don't work to change—these couples fall into a state of enmeshment. Neither scenario has a happy prognosis; working together utilizing this book or guidance from a therapist can help the partners navigate out of their pain into the light of awareness and healing.

The Genesis of the Marital Melodrama: The Primal Wound, the Primary Fear and the Accompanying Key Decision

When partners are engaged in the *marital melodrama*, each has a *primal wound* he or she seeks to heal. The fantasy is that a partner will provide that healing by supplying the nurturing that was not available in infancy and childhood. Again, to avoid confusion, let's refer to the male who fears engulfment and the female who fears abandonment to clarify this idea.

His wound is caused in infancy and early childhood when he is pushing his boundaries and testing the patience of his parents. When he goes too far, he senses that he is the object of parental displeasure, even hostility. Sometimes he is punished, humiliated or abused during these forays into budding selfhood. The primary fear is that "I am unlovable as I am and I am bad if I incur the displeasure of my care-givers." Paradoxically, he also fears being engulfed by parental smothering, because the controlling parent is denying his essence, his core self. Only a prescribed behavior, one that is pleasing or prohibited, is rewarded or punished. When this happens, he decides: "I am not lovable as I am, so I have to give up being me and settle for being approved, admired or pleasing." From this decision, made earlier than conscious memory, comes the adult fear of engulfment: he fears he cannot be himself.

Her primal wound flows from a lack of effective maternal bonding and the inability to form a sense of individual self. The primary fear is that "I cannot exist." She fears being annihilated or banished and this may be accompanied by amorphous dread. Some of the key decisions she makes as a child may be: "I cannot have feelings, so I cannot be." "Feelings are unsafe, but I can do things and take care of others." "I am unlovable, but I can love and do for you." "It's OK if you don't love me; I can love you." These childhood fears and their accompanying decisions form the fertile ground for the adult fear of abandonment.

In adult life, this dread may show up as a black hole, a feeling that *I am nothing, lifeless, banished.* This dreadful emptiness gives rise to the drive to be needed. When she is not needed, she feels abandoned and then gives way to helplessness. When she is needed and her fear of abandonment is at bay, she seems to be super-critical, even enraged, when her partner fails to meet her needs.

The Supporting Cast

Supporting the *marital melodrama* and the two partners are:

- **Shame:** Shame is expressed through embarrassment, withdrawal, avoidance and self-deprecation.
- **Guilt:** Guilt is expressed through rigidity, control, secrecy, self-imposed limits and a highly judgmental inner Critical Parent.
- **Rage:** At the base of rage is fear that as a partner, his specialness has not been recognized or fear that she is not lovable.
- **Perfection:** Perfection is the need to be seen as important and grand. The partner is required to be an equally perfect reflection.

- **Entitlement:** An enlarged sense of entitlement leads to self-righteous claims, game-playing and secret-keeping.
- **Vengeance:** Vengeance wells up from feelings of hate and anger. The partner who feels vengeful will do anything to get even.
- **Envy and Jealousy:** These are both powerful emotions that can lead to a reactive, hateful rage toward the one who is envied.

The Three Acts of the Marital Melodrama

Now that we've discussed the differences between the partner who fears engulfment and the one who fears abandonment, we can view the three acts of this marital drama (as described by Bion in *Experiences in Groups*) with greater understanding.

Act I: Pairing

Pairing involves a shared fantasy about the relationship that sees the similarities, blinds the partners to their differences and supports their magical belief that love will conquer all. When the *marital melodrama* becomes cyclical, the fantasy metamorphoses into a belief that "We can make it because we really love each other, so come, let's try again." This second fantasy maintains the blindness, with the partners still denying their own responsibility. It downplays the differences that need to be understood, replacing that work with the feeling that "If only my partner would change, then everything would be all right." The underlying feeling in this act is expectancy. These partners behave as if love were a separate magical aspect to their marriage that could sustain and save them. This magical love must never be tested, for it will vanish and the relationship will shift to Act II.

> *In chapter 4 we discussed Rob and Andrea, the couple who broke up when Rob's lies, affairs and substance abuse became too obvious and hurtful to deny. Andrea tossed him out at each indiscretion only to take him back when he promised he would change. Their cyclical* marital melodrama *was*

repeated because of their belief in fantasies: Andrea's was that if only Rob would change his ways, their relationship could be saved, while Rob believed he could win Andrea over again and get her to stay with him no matter what he did. In truth, neither of them took responsibility for his or her part in the demise. They entrusted their love and the life of their relationship to an illusion.

Act II: Fight/Flight

By the time partners reach Fight/Flight, each partner's *script* is well rehearsed and he or she behaves as if the other person is fully responsible for the partner's plight. They alternate between fighting with and fleeing from each other. The primary feelings underneath the surface are anger and disappointment. The one who fears abandonment attacks the partner who fears engulfment, criticizing him for not being perfect. He goes into a rage (or collapses) when there is an actual or threatened loss of nurturing resources. This exchange provokes an abandonment crisis to which he responds with passive-aggressive withdrawal. She eventually issues an invitation to return, which he accepts, because the world outside really does not offer him the resources and the care that she does. Thus begins Act III—the phase of Dependence.

Peter and Rebecca, the couple whose youthful attraction was rekindled in mid-life, are good examples of the Fight/Flight response that emerges when reality shatters romantic illusions.

In our last discussion, Peter, whose past includes a criticizing, alcoholic father, and Rebecca, whose mother died when she was young and who went to boarding school, had agreed to reconcile on the condition that Peter would tell Rebecca about the behaviors he found hurtful, but, as disclosed previously, he didn't. Though Peter is by nature a sensitive and caring man, his script *tells him it's not OK to feel those emotions. Thus he has spent his life repressing the highs and lows and creating a safe, even, undisturbed emotional state. Rebecca's script tells her she's not lovable at all, because everyone who*

loved her left when she was so young. She has always reacted
as if she is OK, denying the pain of her losses, creating a "fam-
ily" for herself out of workmates and women friends.

During the first reconciliation, Peter exhibited fear of
engulfment behaviors, blaming Rebecca. As you may recall, he
tried to be caring but recreated the pattern he established with
his father, withdrawing to protect himself. Rebecca sensed his
withdrawal from her and collapsed in pain and fear, because
someone she loved might leave her—again. When she con-
fronted Peter, he responded with confusing passive-aggression.
Their joint behaviors became so painful for both of them that
they finally agreed to break up. A few months later, Rebecca
issued an invitation to return, which Peter accepted, because
he had not found the care she offered in the "outside" world.
Their "Fight/Flight" melodrama continued.

Act III: Dependence

Dependence begins when the partners try again without seeking
help. Both partners sink once more into blind dependency upon each
other. The one who fears engulfment expects the one who fears abandonment to stanch the ache that flows from the primal wound by her
appreciation of him, her admiration of him as being special. She does
the best she can to serve and fulfill that expectation, while internally
seething at his imperfections and failures. These imperfections and failures are, in reality, hers projected onto him. This couple sinks into
denial or resignation to their plight. One of the partners is dominant,
the other submissive, with the resulting relationship at risk of becoming pathological. The primary underlying feelings are hopelessness and
despair.

Betsy and Link, the married couple with a daughter whom we discussed earlier, demonstrated a repetitive pattern of attack and withdrawal that illuminates Act III. Their *marital melodrama* was fueled by
her angry father and his neglectful mother.

Without help, Betsy could not see that in her criticism of
Link's "failures," she was really seeing her own. Without help,
Link could not see that when he withdrew from her attacks, he

was really withdrawing from his mother's attacks. Link eventually sought solace in an ill-fated Internet romance, while Betsy buried herself in work, dulling the pain with gambling, cigarettes and food. They sought counseling briefly, but remained stuck in the painful trap of their hostile-dependent ties. For a while they lived on separate floors of their home, filled with hopelessness and despair. Though Betsy eventually moved away, the feelings remained, until death—quite literally—did them part.

These couples demonstrate the futility, desperation and entrapment that occur when the *marital melodrama* is allowed to replay indefinitely.

The behavior that accompanies the players and their supporting feelings in the *marital melodrama* cannot be trusted. Lines delivered by *script*-driven needs do not convey the real emotion. Only our body language and other non-verbal clues disclose the unconscious intention behind the lines. The *script*-driven communication that characterizes The Politics of Love feeds the anger.

Although the conflict recurs, there is hope. The *marital melodrama* plays out to varying degrees in every relationship. With understanding, willingness and action, the *inner family theater* can be dismantled, allowing our true selves to run the show. Identifying what kind of partner you are in the marriage (one who fears engulfment or one who fears abandonment), which act you are stuck in (Pairing, Fight/Flight or Dependence) and what the driving emotions are (from shame to vengeance) will allow you and your partner to build a pathway to harmony together and to trust that the communication between you is authentic and honest.

Endeavor: Who's on Stage

Overview
This Endeavor will help you get to know and understand the characters of your *inner family theater*. Once you know them, you will be able to manage your emotional life with your partner more successfully. To use this inventory, supply the information or words in the following categories. Again, play your first hunch; do not change your response unless you want to add a remembered piece of information.

Activities
Each partner should take some time alone to reflect and respond to these questions. Write the answers in your notebook, agree on a time and place and then come together and share your responses.

A. **What were my mother's behavioral and verbal messages concerning:**
   1. Marriage?
   2. Treatment of my father?
   3. Her positive characteristics?
   4. Her negative characteristics?
   5. Negative messages I received?
   6. Positive messages I received?

B. **What were my father's behavioral and verbal messages concerning:**
   1. Marriage?
   2. Treatment of my mother?
   3. His positive characteristics?
   4. His negative characteristics?
   5. Negative messages I received?
   6. Positive messages I received?

C. **How do my parents' messages show up in:**
   1. The way I feel and behave in our marriage?
   2. The negative messages and actions I give my partner?
   3. The way I attack, criticize and blame my partner?
   4. The positive messages and actions I give my partner?

As you meet and share your responses, ask questions that bring only clarification and understanding. Remember to make no judgmental or teasing comments. Listen through the words to the feelings and the story being told by your partner. Embarrassment, irritation and reluctance are all normal reactions to this process. Simply release these feelings. Remember to use your Guidelines for Safe Communication. Feel free to shed any tears and ask for support from your partner. If you feel angry or upset with your partner's answers, use "I" messages to convey those feelings (for example: "When you said [whatever it was], I felt [hurt, angry, bewildered, etc.]" rather than "You made me feel…").

Sharing the Process
- What was helpful to you as you learned about your family dynamics?
- What was helpful to you as you learned about your partner's family dynamics?
- What did you learn that you feel applies to your relationship?
- In what ways are the relationships in both sets of parents similar to your relationship?
- In what ways are the relationships in both sets of parents different from your relationship?
- Are there any changes you want to make in your relationship?
- Working together, how could you implement these changes?

Appreciations
- Share one or two focused appreciations of your partner that flow from this Endeavor.
- Talk about one or two ways in which your partner's sharing was important for you.

Close With—
- A warm embrace and—with eye contact—an "I love you."

A Reminder
Continue your Sharing Times, Caring Acts and Courtship Events. Renew your commitment to these activities.

Endeavor: Earning a Starring Role

Overview

When your *script*-driven expectations and demands conflict with your partner's *script*-driven expectations and demands, trouble arises, because there is an unconscious requirement that your partner will satisfy them all. The words we use often do not convey what we are really feeling, but body language and non-verbal clues can disclose unconscious motivation. *Script*-driven communication is the core issue of this Endeavor, because it feeds the angry melodrama between you and your partner. The trouble is that arguments spawned by the melodrama, no matter how they resolve, do not silence the *inner family theater*.

The awareness you have gained thus far and the activities in this Endeavor will help you recognize when you are engaged in a *marital melodrama* and will teach you how to pull the curtain. You will learn to communicate honestly from your true self, instead of from the *script*-driven characters of your past.

Activities

There are three parts to this all-important Endeavor: Part 1: Review your responses to previous Endeavors that have laid the foundation for what follows. Part 2: Use what you have learned to identify key elements in your *inner family theater* and link them to what happens in your relationship. And Part 3 is the solution: Create an agreement that will interrupt your *marital melodrama* and stop its endless and destructive cycle.

Part 1: Understanding Your Marital Melodrama

Separately review your responses to these Endeavors: "Who Wrote This Thing" (chapter 3), "Curtain Up" (chapter 3) and "Behind the Scenes" (chapter 4). Keep them in your mind. Gradually take more responsibility for your own transactions with your partner and avoid blaming, hidden expectations and patterned, recycled arguments.

Part 2: Understanding My Part in Our Marital Melodrama

Now take some time separately to record your responses to this section in your notebook. Then get together and share your responses, taking turns and using your Guidelines for Safe Communication.

1. What were the critical parental messages and critical parental behaviors of my childhood?
2. What were my responses to those? (scared, sad, angry, hurt, compliant, rebellious) Give details.
3. My key childhood decision was…
4. One thing I can do to stop our *marital melodrama* is…

To transcend your *marital melodrama*, you both must…

- Know your own emotional story
- Know your partner's emotional story
- Use your Guidelines for Safe Communication

Part 3: Interrupting Your *Marital Melodrama*

Next, create together an agreement about how you will interrupt and then stop an episode of your *marital melodrama*. Don't focus on your partner unless your partner asks for your help. Focus instead on how *you* will change, using words, changes of behavior and your own sense of growing awareness. Focus on what *you* can do to change your part in the drama. After creating the agreement together, write out the clauses, sign and date it. Make a copy for each partner to keep with your individual notebook.

Sharing the Process

- Share two things you learned about yourself and your partner.
- Were there any surprises?
- Working together, how can you implement your agreement?

Appreciations

- Share two focused appreciations of your partner that flow from the activities in this difficult Endeavor.

- Share one way your partner's participation was important to you.
- Share one thing that had special emotional meaning for you.

Close With—
- A hug and a heartfelt "I love you."

Chapter 8

Trading in Power for Love

Three things in human life are important.
The first is to be kind; the second is to be kind;
the third is to be kind.

Henry James

The work outlined in this chapter will require great courage on the part of you and your partner. Being fully alive to life is a courageous act. Many of us think heroism is only those spectacular acts of bravery that occur amidst great danger. But heroism is also an everyday affair. To be a conscious, responsible, creative human being is to live heroically. For some just getting up in the morning is a heroic act. For others changing jobs, going to school, ending a relationship, surviving on limited funds, managing one or more children alone—all of these are filled with heroism. So, too, is staying in a relationship that isn't rewarding or fulfilling. That is the work of this chapter. Trading in power for love means facing our biggest fears, recognizing the behaviors that are generated by those fears and being willing to respond differently.

In chapter 7 we learned about the importance of cultivating honest communication through self discovery and awareness of your and your partner's *inner family theaters* and the roles they play in your *marital melodrama*. Using your new consciousness, you and your partner can begin the work that will give you both the skills to trade in power for love and thus transcend Stage 2 successfully.

Learning about Power

The first, last and best rule for the lesson you and your mate are learning in this chapter is, as Robert A. Johnson has written in *We: Understanding the Psychology of Romantic Love*, "Where power rules, love perishes." Remember that rule, as it will be the key to stopping the destructive communication and behavior patterns couples resort to during Stage 2.

Power is the capacity to do, to prohibit, to affect or to change. Within a relationship it is the capacity to get someone to do something he or she would not otherwise do. People wield power in many ways, including the use of guilt and shame, money, real or threatened violence, manipulation, lies and deceit, fear, influence, coercion and pleading. These techniques use up not only physical energy, but also fiscal, personal and emotional resources. All power plays are *script*-driven and are used to obtain negative or positive acknowledgment. They exist to maintain and protect early *script* decisions.

Every couple creates a unique arena of power with its own culture, language and special set of triggers and cues. It has its own unwritten rules, unspoken codes of conduct, non-verbal signals and covert understandings. Couples who do not learn to recognize the arena of power they have created become delayed in The Politics of Love—sometimes for years, even decades. These couples sink into hostile-dependency and utilize power in destructive and harmful ways.

A loser in a power struggle is someone who takes risks, fails or falters, then seeks to blame it on someone else. A winner takes risks, fails or falters, then seeks to discover what went wrong and how he or she will do it differently next time. Since **the only relationship that works is**

one on which you and your partner work, your task will be to find out what caused the failure so you can change the outcome next time.

Why Couples Stay Stuck

If you concentrate on what your partner has not done or is not doing, it is received as and feels like criticism or blame, as though you are making him or her responsible for your feelings. Your love seems conditional to your partner. This is a one-down, dependent position and it has consequences. By not accepting responsibility for your own *script*, you condemn yourself and your partner to repeating the past over and over again.

To help you get unstuck, let's look at the seat of all power struggles. Developed by psychiatrist Jim Karpman, the Drama Triangle is a convenient way to see how the scenes in our everyday lives play out. In the triangle there are three roles: Rescuer, Persecutor and Victim. Such roles are masks; they hide the real feelings inside and they exist for the purpose of manipulation. All three roles originate from the Not OK Child and Critical Parent of the *inner family theater*. While most of us fall somewhere on a continuum, there are extreme characteristics of each position:

- The *Rescuer* does more for others than he or she feels good about doing, yet sets it up to nurture the dependence of the other, offering self-righteous help or advice, and then feels resentment, guilt, remorse and fear.
- The *Persecutor* sets unnecessarily strict limits on behavior and enforces the rules but often does so cruelly, even brutally. He or she feels resentful, bitter and angry and blames, attacks, criticizes, defends and finds fault.
- The *Victim* feels sorry for him or herself and is really angry with someone, life or the universe. Feeling fearful, hurt and ashamed, the Victim pouts, stuffs, uses passive-aggression and withdraws.

The scene begins when one partner assumes a role from any one of the three positions. For example, a woman assuming the Rescuer role will do something very helpful for her partner, while inwardly feeling resentful or like a martyr for having to do it. Whether conscious or unconscious, this feeling is enough to trigger the drama, which will escalate until one partner or both partners either withdraw or end up on the therapist's couch or in the courtroom, the hospital or the morgue.

Drama Triangle Dynamics: Driving Emotions and Role Switches

Both partners can change roles during ongoing conflicts. When the emotions of anger, hurt, guilt, resentment, shame and/or fear are felt in the current position, then a role switch is made to a new position.

- Rescuer gives way to Victim when fear that the emotional results sought (e.g., appreciation) will not be forthcoming.
- Victim gives way to Persecutor when resentment becomes the dominant and overriding feeling.
- Persecutor yields to Rescuer when guilt about what one has said or done overwhelms the feelings of resentment.

An argument between Mark and Mary over children's bedtimes illustrates this dynamic. This is the couple who created a blended family of three boys from Mark's previous marriage and one daughter from Mary's previous marriage. Mary's feelings of unworthiness and Mark's fear of abandonment (from their *inner family theaters*) brought them to counseling, where strong commitment delivered new understanding.

> *Mark: "I'm definite about this, Mary. You have to be consistent with kids and mine know that lights out is at nine o'clock every night, no exceptions."*
>
> *Mary: "I know, Mark. But your kids have grown up with that. Sarah hasn't, so it's harder for her to understand why you're being so strict. She just wants to see the last hour of this movie, just this one night. Is that so much to ask?"*
>
> *Mark: "Yes, damn it, it is! Don't you see that Sarah is manipulating you, pushing us both, to see how much of her way she can have? Unless we're firm with her she'll just keep*

pushing. Besides, the rules have to be the same for her as they are for the rest of the family."

Mary: (slipping into Victim) "Well, I guess I'm just the world's worst mom then. I just have so much trouble understanding why you can't be a little more flexible when it comes to my daughter."

Mark: (feeling abandoned and slipping into his own Victim) "God, Mary, I'm not an ogre. I just need you to support me on this, but I guess you don't think it's important enough."

Partners can change these negative dynamics by learning to make these distinctions:

1. *Genuine Help versus playing Rescuer* – Genuine help is given freely with no strings attached, no burden of guilt or obligation and no expectation of return.

2. *Genuine Need versus playing Victim* – Know yourself well enough to understand what you genuinely need. Disclose your feelings, spell out what you want and negotiate to what feels fair.

3. *Genuine Confrontation versus Persecutor* – Give an authentic response, one that reveals your feelings and acknowledges your part in creating the situation (i.e., admit that a *script*-driven response in you caused a certain behavior).

Accepting and developing your own authentic sense of self, experiencing the vulnerability that comes with feeling and hearing honest emotions and negotiating cooperatively with your partner can also help you avoid this negative behavioral pattern. Cooperative negotiation is a four step process.

First – Ask for 100 percent of what you want.

Second – Give genuine and authentic responses.

Third – Know what you can settle for without guilt, anger, fear or resentment.

Fourth – Negotiate for what is felt to be fair.

The keys to avoiding the Drama Triangle are:

No rescues	Be responsible
No lies	Be truthful and authentic
No secrets	Be self-revealing
No power-plays	Be cooperative
No choosing to be victim	Be nonjudgmental

Using these techniques and having worked hard to become more aware of their *script-driven* responses, Mark and Mary resolved their argument about their kids' bedtimes.

Being aware of your and your partner's *inner family theaters* and learning to stay off the Drama Triangle gives couples insight and improves their basic relationship. Now how can you deal with conflict?

Developing a Pathway through Conflict

Yelling, screaming, punching and threatening are not helpful ways through conflict; in fact, they are detrimental. One can choose to be hostile, blaming, even abusive and destructive or one can choose to be cooperative, effective and productive in the resolution of conflict. To resolve important issues you must choose constructive paths. Conflict managed in a constructive and healthy way will bring you to the threshold of a balanced and harmonious relationship.

When partners are engaged in conflict, they get swept up in the power struggle, often bringing the events of their *inner family theaters* into the power arena. Awareness of your *inner family theater* will help you to recognize when you somehow project your own emotional material onto the other partner. While you may be caught up in the fury of the battle, you still can know you are working out your own emotional issues through each other. You can acknowledge your own projections and ambivalence, even as you continue to project. To debrief any *script*-driven battle you must identify your disowned parts and take responsibility for those projections.

When power dominates the relationship, you may have to use power-oriented responses while you seek to change your connections from power to love. Here are strategies you may use while you are metamorphosing your partnership from power struggle to loving negotiation:

1. Know your *script* and take responsibility for it.
2. Trust your intuition.
3. Use the *Inchworm Rule*: Give an inch of vulnerability. If you get an inch of vulnerability returned, then proceed. If not, it is not emotionally safe; do not proceed.
4. Know and follow the *two yes-but* guideline: In any conversation, if you give or get more than two *yes-but*s, you are no longer in a conversation, but in an argument. Your *scripts* will determine the outcome.
5. Omit judgment from your language. Avoid the word "you" in phrases such as "You make me..." or "When you said..." "I thought you were..." or "You are..."
6. Avoid *why* questions. They put the questioner one-up and the one being questioned on the defensive. The why/because dialogue invites power games, adversarial responses and impasse into the struggle.
7. Do not play analyst or teacher to your partner unless requested or you get permission.
8. No teasing—teasing is hostile and sarcasm is merely anger in disguise.
9. Refrain from retaliating or climbing onto the Drama Triangle.
10. Choose to be cooperative (not acquiescent, argumentative or retaliatory).

You can also recognize the inner tension driven by the paradox of needing to be close while needing to be separate. As you begin to know that intimacy and autonomy are not mutually exclusive, you will be able to negotiate desires for both with less intrusion into each other's boundaries. This understanding is not instantaneous. You will begin by learning the phases of this journey and then discover how to move from one to the next.

In *Phase I: Concealed Dependency*, very little distinction is made between you and your partner. There is intense intolerance for separateness while continuous efforts are made to establish total control of the other person. Excessive envy, jealousy, projection, blaming, attacking, defensiveness, withdrawal, anger and fear exist. Blind, *script*-driven patterns characterize partner transactions.

Phase II: Gaining Awareness of Separateness is a time of chaos and learning when there is an awakening of some understanding of yourself and your partner; however, there is still very little differentiation between each other and only a dim awareness that you cannot really fulfill each other's needs. *Script*-driven needs still run the relationship, but there is a growing awareness of external boundaries and the futility of blame and criticism. You begin to see the value of each other.

In *Phase III: Connected and Healthy Interdependence*, you each begin to accept responsibility for your own inner conflicts. As each partner comes to understand that the other is different, both develop more tolerance and understanding of each other. You begin to share dreams and take responsibility for your own psychological dynamics. Frustration is more easily accepted and the need for continuing guided partnership work is realized.

Now that you know the phases, you can take four steps to progress from Phase I to Phase III.

First, identify and resonate with your own story. In this step, it is important not to get discouraged; things will often seem to get worse before they get better. Create a *no-exit relationship*—a place where growth and development can flourish. As the name implies, this is an agreement between both partners that no matter what happens emotionally, neither person will walk out on the other or on the marriage. It means that, barring illegal or violent behaviors, you won't abandon the scene just because it's painful or uncomfortable. Once a no-exit promise is made, both partners can feel safe to think the unthinkable and face the terrors within. Each of you can own your own *script* and take responsibility for it. Both can look at the struggles within yourselves, as well as the struggles in the relationship.

Second, recognize and concede there is a better way. This requires that both of you work through issues, including identifying and releasing past hurts. You and your partner reengage trust and enhance your negotiation skills to enable both of you to work through your personal *script* issues and your *marital melodrama*.

Third, reframe the relationship. This step is essential, though not easy. The relationship needs to be freed of *script*-driven connections and reborn through understanding, empathy, renewed courtship and appreciation of the unique needs of yourself, your partner and your relationship. This takes thoughtfulness, kindness, time, energy, trust, patience and perseverance.

Fourth, release the past and embrace the future. Now you both must take responsibility for your own *script*-driven needs and not hold your partner responsible for pleasing you. Embrace the paradox that by releasing your own needs you receive more of what you seek. More importantly, you will discover that mature love is anchored in the ability to give love, receive love and *stay the course.*

Understanding Anger in Relationships

One of the most commonly misunderstood emotions is anger. The way in which you handle anger has a great impact on your interpersonal relations, your success in the world and your ability to mobilize personal power. *Script*-driven communication often contains anger and feeds the angry conflict between partners. When the related emotional issues are decoded, anger can become an important resource used to renew the relationship.

Anger in such situations is of two kinds. The first is a reaction to chronic and repeated negligence of real obligations by others. It is a reaction to disappointment and hurt, rooted in current circumstances. This kind of anger, when delivered constructively, helps reassert one's sense of dignity and self-respect.

The second kind of anger is much more common and destructive. Its goal is to hide fear and replace hurt. It is associated with depression and reveals a sense of impotence and helplessness. Whether it is loud, chronic temper-tantrums, whining, chronic complaining or screaming, ranting and raving, this behavior on the part of one partner is meant to change the behavior of the other and avoid taking responsibility for one's own existence. Such expressions, laden with threats and intimidation, are full of hidden, deep-seated hurts. Angry outbursts produce bitterness and reactive anger that may be either shown or hidden away, lying in wait for some way to express itself.

Even when anger is authentic, it is not best used for corrective intervention. Our feelings of anger are unreliable as guides to reality until fully released and understood. It is much wiser to *cool down* before making any decisions or taking any action.

However, when we *stuff down* or stifle anger, suppressing all signs of it, undesirable effects occur. People who regularly stuff down anger have a greater tendency toward high blood pressure, ulcers and heart attacks. If we suppress anger long enough, we may lose touch with the feeling entirely and become unable to mobilize our full personal power. Anger can turn passive-aggressive and sabotage the desires of others when there are unexpressed resentments. Chronic lateness, forgetting commitments, procrastination and other similar behaviors all hide the real problems and usually leave the issue unresolved.

Long-unexpressed anger turns into deeply held resentments. A person who harbors resentments usually has relatively little Nurturing Parent available and may behave in mean, even abusive, ways to others and to him- or herself. To maintain intimacy and trust, anger must find appropriate expression; this is one of very few things that are certain and predictable in human relations. Couples who do not express anger appropriately over time become ever more distant and have more and more difficulty being intimate. Finally, they lose all access to intimacy between them, though they may continue to live together. They succumb to a life of intimate estrangement from one another.

Displays of anger violate strong social taboos. They can restimulate fear caused by childhood abuse or past fights with partners where anger escalated into emotionally or physically hurtful outcomes. If fear occurs, you will need time to diffuse it. In order to decrease the fear around the expression of anger, two ideas are useful:

- Anger need not escalate; it can be managed.
- Appropriate expression of anger de-escalates and diffuses it: when we express anger safely, we are less likely to act it out.

The safe release of anger removes the potential for hurt. The expression of anger in an appropriate manner is positive and needs to be perceived that way by partners. When it is safely expressed, safely heard, accompanied by each person owning his or her own *script* and followed by reconnection and forgiveness, anger provides an opportunity to realize deeper intimacy and more profound growth. With every conflict, partners in a coupled relationship come that much closer to achieving *emotional literacy*.

One way fighting can be accomplished constructively is to develop some Guidelines for Fair Fighting. Guidelines are just that. No one is perfect and no one can remember them all the time, especially in the heat of battle. Yet it is important to commit to these guidelines and to make a genuine effort to abide by them. Do not, however, use them as additional weapons to find the other person wanting, defective or Not OK if he or she strays from using them. The goal is to use these guides authentically, cooperatively and well. They should be tailor-made by each couple.

Hopefully, you have worked intensely on the issues illuminated in this chapter. As I said at the beginning, this work requires courage and faith. You have learned what keeps you stuck in the power struggle and the tools you can use to transcend it. Your new strategies for resolving conflict, managing anger and fair fighting allow you to dethrone the rule of power and enthrone the rule of love in your relationship.

Endeavor: Mad about You

Overview

Anger has many faces. It lurks behind hurt or it can hide the hurt. It may be explosive, frightening, out of control. It might be passive-aggressive. Anger accompanies us every day. It knots people's stomachs in the face of everyday frustrations like slow elevators, traffic snarls, long supermarket lines, annoying drivers or rude, abrasive teenagers. In addition, it occurs in primary relationships when one partner does not meet the other's expectations, demands or perceived rights. When one partner believes that this is happening, his heart rate increases, his blood pressure rises and the adrenalin pump begins. Her jaw muscles tighten. The fight-or-flight response is triggered.

Learning to manage your anger and hostility in healthy ways is important to the survival of a meaningful partnership. If you work, you can develop skills to counter tendencies toward the inappropriate expression of anger. You can learn a broad range of responses that will decrease the risks to your bodily health and bring more kindness, love and patience to your partnership.

The activities in this Endeavor are designed to give you a more complete understanding of how each partner's anger works so you can do something about it. First, take an inventory that will help identify your anger patterns and expressions. Next, look at how it works in your marriage. Finally, identify ways to release the anger and build a healthier connection with your partner.

Activities

A. Learning about Your Anger: A Questionnaire

Take some time separately to reflect and respond to the following statements or questions in your individual notebooks. Come back together and share your responses, one topic at a time. Remember to use the Guidelines for Safe Communication you and your partner have created.

1. Anger is…
2. When you were growing up, how did your mother show her anger?

3. When you were growing up, how did your father show his anger?

4. As a child, how did you show your anger?

5. What do you do or say when you are angry with your partner?

6. Are you satisfied with how you handle and resolve your anger with your partner?

7. Describe the changes you would like to make in how you express and resolve anger.

8. Describe the changes you would like your partner to make in how he or she expresses and resolves anger.

B. The Anger Limits Questionnaire

It is essential to designate the limits of acceptable and unacceptable words and behavior during a fight. In your own notebook specify your limits in clear and precise terms. Define the limits you would like your partner to live by as well. Be as clear and as simple as you can and be sure you identify what is truly important for you. Cover such areas as physical behavior, voice tone, threats and ending a fight. Avoid the temptation to use this exercise as another way to control your partner.

1. For me, during a fight, it is acceptable to do and say...

2. For me, during a fight, it is not acceptable to do and say...

3. For my partner, during a fight, it is acceptable to do and say...

4. For my partner, during a fight, it is not acceptable to do and say...

Take turns sharing your responses with each other.

C. Our Fair Fight Guidelines

Based on what you have learned about how you deal with anger, how you respond to anger and what is and is not acceptable, create your list of Fair Fight Guidelines. Together come up with at least three guidelines, but not more than ten, that will make disagreements safe and productive for you both. Write them on a separate page in each of your notebooks. When you have finished, make sure both sets of guidelines are identical, then sign each other's. Review and revise these guidelines from time to time.

Sharing the Process

- Did you learn anything about yourself and your partner that will be helpful to you when you engage in *marital melodrama*?
- Were there any surprises about the way you view anger and the way you fight?
- Were there any surprises about the way your partner views anger and the way he or she fights?
- How do you feel about creating your Fair Fight Guidelines?
- Share with each other any other thoughts about what you learned and how you feel this applies to your relationship.

Appreciations

- Each of you confide one or two focused appreciations of your partner that flow from listening to him or her during this activity.
- Each partner tell the other one way your partner's participation was important for you.

Close With—

- True appreciation of what a wonderful effort you each made in this Endeavor— with a long, warm embrace and a tender "I love you."
- Finally, decide together what you would enjoy doing in celebration of completing this challenging Endeavor—a night out, a weekend away, a quiet walk or a special coffee break at your favorite café.

Endeavor: Stopping the Show

Overview

You have worked hard thus far to discover your *inner family theaters*, to become aware of the *scripts* that run your lives and to understand the actions or emotions such as fear, embarrassment, shame, anger, hurt or guilt that trigger the dramatic conflict in your relationship. In this Endeavor, you will focus on the dynamic between you when both *scripts* are in play. Once you are acquainted with your roles, the way they change places and the feelings that go with them, you can stop the show. You can step out of the dark conflict and transform your marriage into one that shines.

The way off the Drama Triangle is to be authentic and courteous. Be conscious of your *script*, your *inner family theater*, your part in your *marital melodrama* and your role in the Drama Triangle. Take responsibility for your behavior and refrain from making your partner responsible for your feelings. These changes take time to establish, but if you both are willing, you can do it.

This activity will move you from a conflicted relationship and into the clean, clear, healthy relationship you both deserve. Each of you should take time apart to study the characteristics, behaviors and skills and to answer the questions in your notebook. Then come together in the usual way to share your responses, one partner at a time. Your goal is to discover how you can apply your new-found knowledge to your relationship so that you can each move from Rescuer, Persecutor and Victim to the caring, assertive and vulnerable partner you can become.

Activities

A. Genuine Help: The Caring Partner
- does not take over unless asked
- always uses respect
- is empathic and compassionate
- senses genuine need

Respond to the following in your notebooks:
   1.   One way I show genuine care for my partner is...

2. Which behaviors of the caring partner describe me best?
3. How can I become a more caring partner?

B. Genuine Confrontation: The Assertive Partner

- asks for what he or she wants
- says "no" to what he or she doesn't want
- gives safe feedback, initiates negotiation
- makes changes to get his or her needs met

Respond to the following in your notebooks:

1. Which behaviors of the assertive partner describe me best?
2. One way I can be more assertive with my partner is...
3. One way I would like my partner to be more assertive with me is...

C. Genuine Need: The Vulnerable Partner

- thinks through the predicament from an adult perspective
- uses both cognitive abilities and emotional literacy for problem-solving

Respond to the following in your notebooks:

1. How do I want my partner to connect with me when I am feeling vulnerable?
2. One specific way I will improve my problem-solving skills is...

Sharing the Process

- Share one thing you learned about how conflict works in your relationship.
- Share one thing about yourself you would like to change.
- Share one way this Endeavor has brought greater understanding of your partner.
- Share one way you can move from conflict to positive interactions.

Appreciations
- Give your partner a heartfelt appreciation for the hard work he or she has done in completing this Endeavor.
- Do any other particularly meaningful appreciations flow from this Endeavor?

Close With—
- A warm embrace and well-deserved "I love you."

Endeavor: Money Madness

Overview

Each partner brings a different experience of money from his or her family history. One partner may have been taught the value of frugality and fiercely defend his or her right to have his or her own bank account; another may be irresponsible about managing money and allow bills to slide, accounts to be overdrawn and credit to lapse. Money may have been used for control or as a punishment or reward. It may have been scarce. Money often becomes a source of marital war as the language of rights, expectations and demands meets the language of attack, blame and defend.

This Endeavor will help you to gain an understanding of your childhood orientation toward money and to see how it creates melodrama in your relationship. You and your partner will then develop a cooperative understanding about how to manage money in your home that satisfies both of your needs.

Activities

A. Learning about Your Money Issues: A Questionnaire

This set of questions will help you understand how you developed your attitudes about money. It will help you identify how those attitudes affect you now. Finally, it will encourage you to express your feelings about money today. Be sure you put down your first thought.

1. Money is…
2. When you were growing up, what did your mother do and say about money?
3. When you were growing up, what did your father do and say about money?
4. As a child, what did you decide about money?
5. Are you satisfied with how you and your partner handle and resolve money issues?
6. What do you do when you and your partner disagree about money?

7. What do you want to change so you can feel better about how you and your partner resolve issues about money? Identify the changes you are willing to make and those you would like your partner to make.

Now come together and, taking turns, share your answers.

B. Developing Your Agreement about Money

In your relationship with your partner, it is essential to make clear what is acceptable and what is unacceptable during discussions about money. Keep your responses simple, yet be sure you identify what is truly important for each of you. Now respond to these statements on a separate page in your notebooks:

1. Identify your irritations, hopes, fears and appreciations about how you and your partner handle money.
2. How do you think money should be used in your relationship?
3. Specify the limits about money for yourself and your partner. Be sure you cover such areas as savings, expenditures, money you each get to spend and how you make decisions about money.
4. What are your absolute limits?

Now come together and, taking turns, share your answers.

C. Your Money Page

Develop a money sheet that lists the things to which you have both agreed about the way you will handle money in your relationship. It will serve as a guide when it comes to making future choices and will keep money issues from coloring the rest of your relationship. Write this agreement in your notebooks or on a separate piece of paper and be sure you each have a copy of it. Your Money Page should include a guiding theme, limitations, permissions, goals, a plan, first steps, delegations and other agreements. Sign and date the agreement.

Sharing the Process
- Were there any surprises?
- Did you gain more understanding of each other's issues concerning money?
- Were you able to work out an amicable agreement about money?

Appreciations
- Share one special appreciation for your partner concerning how he or she shared ideas about money.
- Give your partner a focused appreciation about your new approach to money.

Close With—
- A big "Whew, we did it!"
- A big hug and a huge "I love you!"
- Go out on a date with your partner and take satisfaction that you now are working through a tough place in your marriage.

PART III:
TRUE LOVE'S REWARDS

Chapter 9

Developing Harmony Together:
Commitment and Sensuality

*Commitment in a relationship serves as a
container, a structure that surrounds the
thoughts and feelings that are generated in
a relationship.*

Jane G. Goldberg

A vital marriage is a work of art composed by partners that brings zest, replenishment, creativity and meaning to both their lives. Finding the ability and the commitment to express the full spectrum of human emotions safely and constructively will enrich a marriage or partnership, bring the relationship to life and provide full and rewarding intimacy.

In the first two parts of this book, you and your partner learned about the illusion of romance and the chaos it brings; you discovered your *inner family theaters* as well as the perils of the marital drama caused by the conflict between you. Hopefully you both now recognize that the relationship itself needs as much attention as do the partners in it and that *when power rules, love perishes*. If you have taken up the challenge and faced your worst fears, it has been an arduous, sometimes painful journey. Now you and your partner are ready for love's rewards.

In this chapter, we'll begin to put together all the work you have done. We'll look at the meaning of real commitment and learn to recognize boredom and other signs of trouble. You and your partner will develop a new and more conscious method of communicating with each other. Forging a pathway through conflict, the two of you can reach its rewarding resolution. Finally, we will explore the weighty element of sensuality in detail.

Review the five fundamental elements of a successful relationship—friendship, compatibility, affection, commitment and sensuality. Friendship requires active listening skills, harmonious balance between work and play, amenable helpfulness and willing cooperation. Compatibility involves complementary interests, considerate autonomy and personal integrity. Affection entails liking and enjoying your partner, sensitive touching, gracious appreciation and intimate sharing. Commitment calls for intention sustained by conscious choice and anchored in trust, loyalty and reliability. Sensuality requires fondness, fidelity and devotion to consummate physical harmony and balance. When these five elements are present and nurtured, the life of the relationship is ensured. Two of them—commitment and sensuality—deserve a closer look.

On Commitment

Commitment is the glue of a marriage and is an intentional bond between the partners. This intentional bond is a choice derived from hope and founded upon trust. Commitment is about creating the no-exit marriage we talked about in chapter 8. If two emotionally literate partners make a conscious commitment to each other, then it will sustain the partnership through the waxing and waning of the other four elements. Merle Shain wrote these wise words about commitment:

> *I don't know where we got the idea that it is an either/or situation, that it's freedom or commitment, personal growth or responsibility, and that if we choose commitment it will be our loss and not our gain. Because one grows in commitment, one*

doesn't diminish—in fact, it is the only way to grow. And if you commit to nothing but yourself, you pour yourself into the thirsty distance, having nothing to show for it but the cancers on your soul. And you learn too late, as many people have, that man is a ladder, and each rung that takes us higher is a responsibility accepted gratefully, and that there is no personal growth without responsibility, and no such thing as freedom without commitment, nor can there ever be.

The wonderful news is that when we commit, when we co-create a safe and nurturing relationship, we are freer than we've ever been. "Commitment isn't giving something up," says Merle Shain, "it is becoming something more, and as such, it is its own reward."

Signs of Trouble

Commitment is tested at the first sign of trouble. Malaise, ennui, boredom, excuses for absence, reluctance to share time and feeling the excitement has gone from life are only a few of the warning signs of trouble in a marriage. What if the partnership feels stagnant and drab, unrewarding and even boring? When these feelings dominate the partnership, it is a signal there are deep issues that need to be faced but have instead been papered over with denial and avoidance. Anger is repressed, fear is denied and hurt feelings are not worked through.

The price of this repression is the death of the marriage. Desperation leads to withdrawal, depression or flight into a search for excitement, diversion or affairs. Disenchantment and a broken heart are the harvest of failure to recognize a marriage in trouble and in need of loving attention. Couples who lack awareness and settle into an unconscious and emotionally illiterate contract will remain arrested.

A couple we have not discussed before, Harriet and Michael were in a hostile-dependent marriage of thirty years. Michael was large and powerful, but tractable, often silent and unresponsive. He suffered Harriet's outbursts of abusive words and violent actions for years. Once, she threw a log (used for their fireplace) at him and injured his arm and shoulder. That time the police were called, charges were filed and Harriet was required to attend an anger management seminar and to undergo counseling. In spite of the abuse, this couple intended to spend the rest of their lives together. However, they were stuck in a hostile-dependent relationship. They had not been able to develop beyond moderating the violence. Their mutual blindness to their tragic alliance merely seemed like commitment. Unless they get help, a return to abuse could occur.

While not all couples remain stuck like Michael and Harriet, many couples do experience discontent and a seeming lack of fulfillment. They usually blame this on their partners, so they seek excitement outside the marriage. They buy new things, drink more alcohol, abuse drugs, look for boy-toys or trophy girls. Some search for true romance or a soulmate in a fairy tale that soon disintegrates. And yet, they stay married. What is displayed by these marriages is not commitment but rather a co-dependent relationship.

If the relationship is to escape these repetitive, compulsive features, it is essential to recognize the importance of both partners becoming emotionally literate and learn to manage feelings. The process is life-long. Once committed to it, you and your partner will become willing to take responsibility for your own emotional lives in the marriage, allowing you to transcend the *inner family theaters* and put an end to the *marital melodrama.*

Managing Feelings Resourcefully

Feelings like loneliness, anger, shame, guilt, fear and sadness may be difficult to manage safely in a relationship, but it is possible to develop a method to deal with such emotions in a constructive manner. This method will help you and your partner to better recognize where problems are likely and to manage emotions. The commitment to use these techniques will renew, sustain and enhance the developing mature love and intimacy between you.

Most people do not know *what* they feel because they often do not know *that* they feel. Thus, the first step in managing your feelings resourcefully is to become aware of them and how they work. There are three aspects of feelings that are important to know: (1) the feeling itself, (2) the somatic or bodily expression related to the feeling and (3) the behavior expressing the emotion. To manage these aspects of your emotions you need to learn and practice the process that Marshall Sashkin in *Dealing with Feelings: Interpretive Guide* called *The Three R's: Receive, Reflect, Respond.*

Receive means you observe, listen to and see a stimulus that directly impacts you. You do not respond; you simply receive the communication and, when necessary, clarify the situation. This can be done by using *active listening*. Active listening means restating in your own non-judgmental words what you hear another person expressing. Read your partner's facial expression and body language.

Reflect means not acting immediately, but rather assessing and understanding your feelings first. It is helpful here to consider your *script* and understand how it contributes to your predicament. Proper reflection also requires learning to decode the feelings of your partner. You must assess what is the most appropriate response so that each of you can be a willing, tolerant listener with whom the other can talk through feelings and problem-solve effectively.

Respond means to act. There are four possible ways to respond. First, say and do nothing; second, act directly on your feelings. For example, if you are angry, you yell and fight; if you are afraid, you flee or cower. Third, express your feelings with emotionally safe words and ways. Fourth, take some action that is well thought out and takes into account the consequences of your actions. Only options three and four are helpful and sound.

The goal of *The Three R's* is to ensure that you take responsibility for each phase of your emotional process—from receipt of the message to assessing your feelings. Only then can you respond effectively. It is of paramount importance to use *I* messages that take responsibility for feelings and behaviors as in "I feel..."; "I want..."; "I saw..." or "I did...." Refrain from using *you* messages that blame or accuse as in "You are..."; "You made me..."; "You always..." or "You never...."

To fully appreciate the value of learning how to use the principals of *The Three R's*, you will recall Bruce and Nancy, the couple we first met in chapter 4, when their storybook marriage ended in a bitter divorce. We returned to their story in chapter 6 when, four years after their divorce, they rediscovered their love, began to date again and eventually talked of remarrying. This risk frightened them both, so they decided to work through their fears with a counselor.

> *In the sessions that preceded their new wedding date, Bruce and Nancy became emotionally literate. They learned to use effective communication skills and to take responsibility for their own emotional material without projecting it onto each other. They had healed and forgiven their past hurts, anger and disappointments. They understood that love has a dark side and that loyalty, commitment and perseverance can restore the light so long as kindness and thoughtfulness are present.*
>
> *As the day of their wedding grew closer, Bruce suddenly admitted that he was withholding "2 percent" of his love and commitment so he wouldn't be hurt again. Nancy agreed that she, too, was withholding "2 percent." With guidance, it soon became apparent to both that to quantify love and commitment was absurd. They realized that each would be hurt if the marriage did not work, but that to quantify the depth of that hurt was simply not possible. They came to know that no withholding in any percentage would protect them from that hurt; by withholding this mythical "2 percent" they would set the stage for the re-emergence of their* marital melodrama *and thus defeat their efforts to create a whole, loving marriage. From there, it was a small step for each partner to take the full risk—to give fully the love, commitment and loyalty needed to make what was already in their hearts a reality. Many of their friends and family wondered if it would last.*

In a later chapter, we will visit Bruce and Nancy one final time and discover whether their reconciliation succeeded.

As we conclude this all-important section, it is important to remember that, when confronted by trouble in the relationship, your ability to overcome the problem is dependent on your level of commitment. Commitment is supported by willingness to take responsibility for yourselves and for creating cooperation, health and balance in the relationship and to deal with conflict and hostility in healthy ways.

With that knowledge in hand, we can address one of the most powerful components of relationships—sex and sensuality.

On Sensuality

Sensuality acknowledges the importance of sexuality in a way that requires mutual understanding and respect. To the extent that you can surrender to your sexual feelings, your emotional and physical health will improve, for as you surrender to sexual feelings, you also surrender to feelings of love, to the need to be touched by and connect with another human being.

The cultivation of true sensuality, however, means taking responsibility not only for your own sexuality but also for sexually balancing and complementing your partner. Sensual partners are not concerned about equal rights but rather about shared experiences. They seek means to make each other feel good rather than to control each other. Sex can be given as a gift to a partner and appreciated as such. This requires that each person know him- or herself well and that both are willing, courageous and vulnerable enough to share hidden aspects of themselves with their partners. When you and your partner overcome your individual demands, requirements and expectations, each of you can focus instead on using warm, intimate feelings to support the connection between you. Sexual sharing then becomes another expression of love.

Steady conquest of *script*-driven behavior is essential to healthy sensuality. Fully sensual men and women take responsibility for their feelings—whether anger, envy, lust or love. They can form bonds of love and trust with their partners, because they are in touch with their unconscious and relatively free of defense mechanisms. They make efforts to work through conflicts and succeed because of this basic trust. Enjoying sensuality entails using your true feelings constructively, not warding them off.

In addition to the early childhood decisions that are crucial to defining your self-image and self-esteem, you have made decisions concerning your sexuality based upon what you heard and saw as a child. It is important to ferret out this information so that your life and marriage are no longer driven by decisions that never worked.

> *In chapter 1 we met Rebecca and Peter, middle-aged lovers who were delighted to find love at their age and then were rocked by an inexplicable breakup before the first year was out. In chapters 6 and 7, we returned to their story as they were reconciling and breaking up again in a seemingly endless repetition of the Fight/Flight syndrome. Determined to put an end to the pain and see more clearly what was creating this conflict, Rebecca sought counseling and made long strides toward understanding the early childhood decisions that don't work for her in adulthood. She came to recognize the influence of her womanizing father, who had an inappropriate desire for women much too young for him. During their third reconciliation, Rebecca agreed to indulge Peter's desire to "dress her up" in sexy lingerie. When Peter presented her with an outfit, she fell apart, feeling it was too skimpy, gaudy and risqué; Rebecca's reaction was shock, hurt, then anger. Keeping her feelings to herself, she waited until she was alone to sort through her surprisingly strong reaction.*

In this scenario, Rebecca, who had projected the anger and disgust she felt towards her father onto Peter, was willing to look at another reason for her volatile reaction to Peter's innocent gift. However, recall from earlier chapters that Rebecca was also afraid of being abandoned. Without the assurance of a long-term commitment, which Peter was unwilling to give, Rebecca did not feel safe enough to wear the outfit and they were denied the joy of greater intimacy, fulfillment and fun in their sexual relationship.

Using Sex to Serve Other Needs

As Hajcak and Garwood observed in *Hidden Bedroom Partners*, sex is used often to serve purposes other than the pleasure derived from intimate sharing between partners. If you use sex to serve other purposes, it is important to know what those purposes are, understand them and accept responsibility for them.

Table 2
REASONS PEOPLE SOMETIMES USE SEX

Avoiding intimacy, loneliness or boredom	To assuage jealousy
Atonement for guilt	As a refuge
Safeguarding fidelity	To please
Confirming sexual desirability	To buffer depression
Confirming self-esteem	Release stress
Masking anger	To rebel
To achieve dominance or obtain control	Seeking revenge

Sex can be used for varied purposes, which are often hidden from one's partner. In addition to the reasons listed in Table 2, fear of disapproval, a fight or abandonment may lead partners to give sex when they don't feel like it. Partners may give sex to get love or pretend to give love to get sex. In these instances, sex is used manipulatively and exploitatively. If you and your partner can instead be clear as to your motivations for sex, then these reasons can be addressed and otherwise hidden needs disclosed. This will enable both of you to get those needs met more directly or in other ways.

All our lives we've been cautioned not to mistake sex for love. Obvious as that advice may be, the differences may not be. In Table 3, love and sex are contrasted.

Love is intangible. It is an intentional choice we make every day, not a state directed by unconscious needs. Sex, when it comes from a nurturing and caring place, replenishes love. The rewards of cultivating an honest and healthy sexual life are far-reaching. Sex can enhance companionship and affection. It can build self-esteem and set the stage for emotional intimacy.

In the two Endeavors that follow—"Arrivals and Departures" and "Try a Little Tenderness"—you will learn to recognize the ways in which you are or are not present for your marriage and how to re-commit to being and staying there. You'll also discover your sexual *script* and learn how to turn mere sex into a true and tender art form.

Table 3
LOVE AND SEX CONTRASTED

SEX	LOVE
Hormone driven	Not anchored in physiology
Seated in physical connection	Physical contact not required
Global and random	Specific and selective
Selection is indiscriminate	Choice is discriminate
Goal: release of sexual tension	Goal: closeness and intimacy
Physical need quenched through coitus	Emotional closeness realized
Can be coerced and manipulated	Voluntarily given and received
Periodic and short-lived in duration	Committed and enduring
Commences in adolescence and ends with physical decline	Generated by choice and continues by choice

Endeavor: Arrivals and Departures

Overview
Each partner in a marriage has ways of staying in the marriage and ways of leaving the marriage, both literally and figuratively. Major departures include suicide, divorce, murder and mental illness. Daily secondary departures may be such things as working late or compulsively, watching television incessantly, going off in a pout, blaming, withholding, criticizing, getting even or passive-aggressive behavior.

The goals of this Endeavor are to

1. Help you to identify your distinctive ways of staying and leaving.
2. Clarify your partner's ways of staying and leaving.
3. Help you decide how you can re-commit to arriving and staying.

Among the feelings that help you arrive in your marriage are the hope that your needs will be met, a desire to truly give love, genuine caring, the wish to deepen and enrich what you have, willingness to meet your partner's safe sexual needs and desires, a deeper spiritual connection and a readiness to satisfy your partner's needs for touching and affection. Among the fears that encourage departures are the fear of engulfment, fear of being hurt, fear of loss (so you leave first) and a host of others. Departure may also be inspired by anger triggered by not getting what you feel you deserve, being abandoned emotionally, betrayal or any number of other disappointments.

Activities
Each partner should take some time alone to write your responses in your notebooks. Then come together and, taking turns, share them with one another.

1. **How Do I Arrive and Depart?**
    a. Feelings that help me *arrive* in my marriage are…
    b. Ways I *leave* my marriage are…
    c. Ways I *stay* in my marriage are…

2. **What Will I Change?**
    a. Departures I will eliminate are...
    b. Some new ways I will arrive in our marriage are...

Sharing the Process
*   Reflecting over your arrivals and departures, did you become better acquainted with the nature of commitment to your partner?

Appreciations
*   Share any appreciations you have of your partner that flow from these activities.
*   Give an appreciation to your partner concerning his or her commitment to "staying the course" in the marriage.

Close With—
*   Dessert!

Endeavor: Try a Little Tenderness

Overview

Having sex is different from making love. Making love is what happens between orgasms. It involves enjoying each other sensually and being comfortably erotic. It includes thoughtful gestures, kindly words, glances, hugs, kisses, petting, caresses and intercourse. Really enjoying lovemaking means celebrating every stage of sex from the first invitation, glance or spark to the release of orgasms and finally to sharing the joy of the afterglow. Sex is no one's right or duty. Everyday courting is the beginning and ending of lovemaking and from time to time may lead to a sexual encounter.

Whether sex is talked about or ignored in your marriage, your sex lives profoundly influence how you and your partner feel about each other and the marriage. A sensual and satisfying sexual connection nurtures each partner and produces positive feelings about the marriage, thereby strengthening it.

The best sex occurs when you have each become comfortable with your own and your partner's sexuality and learned to let your sexual feelings surface naturally. This comfort deepens your feelings, increases satisfaction and fosters the desire for sex. Accepting and trusting one another encourages you each to risk more and give more. Wonderful sex comes from both partners knowing their own specialness is respected and cherished by the other.

The goal of this Endeavor is to transform your individual searches for sexual gratification into mutual fulfillment.

Activities

1. Sex Talk

In your separate notebooks, respond to the following questions.

1. What were the messages you learned about sex?
2. What did your mother say about sex?
3. What did your father say about sex?
4. What did your mother do about sex?

5. What did your father do about sex?
6. Have you adapted any of their messages into your beliefs and behaviors?
7. What messages/information did you get about sex during your teen years?
8. What messages/information did you get about sex from your church or other religious setting?
9. How about from extended family, neighbors and friends?
10. Any secrets, embarrassments or fears you are willing to share?
11. Any traumatic incidents you will risk sharing?
12. Do you sometimes bring guilt, anger or fear into your sexual life?
13. Do any of these messages get in the way of your lovemaking? If so, how?

Now come together and, taking turns, share what you have written with each other.

2. **The Art of Making Love**
   a. Take some time separately and respond in your notebooks: What do I need in regard to listening, courting, foreplay and sex? Be forthright about hygiene needs, kinds of sex, what feels good, what doesn't, what you are willing to do and what you are not willing to do. Now come together and share this kindly with each other.
   b. Plan a time once or twice a month when you come together and trade gentle massages—ask for what you want in regard to touch and pressure. Aside from asking for what you want and checking what your partner wants, make this a silent activity. Be prepared and set the stage. Use candles, soft music and oil or lotion.
   c. Plan a time when you will come together in a safe setting and verbally share a sexual fantasy with your partner. You can create a fantasy between you or exchange fantasies with each other. Express the manner in which you would appreciate

being touched during the sharing. For example, "Will you please gently stroke my hair and back as I share my fantasy?" If you are unsure about how to touch your partner, ask. For example, "May I massage your feet while you share your fantasy with me?"

d. Plan a time to come together. Set the scene—sit face to face, make eye contact and, while sharing how deeply you feel about your partner, gently touch one another all over. If it feels comfortable, unforced and welcome, enjoy making love using all your new knowledge and skills.

3. The Love Letter

Each partner should take some time separately and write a love letter to your partner that flows from your experience with this Endeavor. Use this list as a guide and include additional thoughts and feelings if you choose.

a. Write about the insights you have gained from doing these activities.

b. Write about how you will change from what you have learned.

c. Write how you value and appreciate your partner sensually and sexually.

d. Write one hope you have for the future of your partnership.

e. Close with one way you will honor your partner in the future.

When you are both ready, come back together and read your letters to each other. For reassurance you may want to touch and hold each other.

Sharing the Process

- Share one important discovery you made about yourself and your partner.
- Any scary moments that you want to share?

Appreciations

- Appreciate two very special qualities in your partner.
- Appreciate two very special qualities in yourself.

- Appreciate the energy and dedication you are both contributing to this work together.

Close With—

- Dinner in a cozy corner of a romantic restaurant where you can share your favorite dessert. Or stay at home and create a sensual setting—light a fire, set out candles, put on some music and prepare a special meal together. Share it. Then make love—slowly, tenderly, with heartfelt joy.

Chapter 10

The Principle of Intentional Love: Perseverance and Transcendence

True love is not a feeling by which we are overwhelmed.
It is a committed, thoughtful decision.

M. Scott Peck

In earlier chapters, you learned how to identify and work through conflict, to embrace the ideal of commitment, to understand the rewards of sensuality and to communicate more effectively. As you and your partner draw closer to achieving a true, mature and intentional marriage, those goals remain constant. Their attainment requires an even closer look at the emotions that drive the two of you.

Intentional, mature love rests on developing an awareness of your own emotional life, developing tools to process these emotions and then applying them both in your marriage. In this chapter you and your partner will examine some additional ways to remain aware of your emotions so you can process and manage them well. Next you will learn how to apply the *principle of intentional love: Mature and devoted love is a conscious choice that—through the practice of respect, responsibility and humility—can transcend the illusion of romance and transform relationships.*

Expression of Emotions

Society sends many early childhood messages that oppose open expression of feelings. Advertisements, movies and television programs encourage us to take alcohol and other drugs or to "keep a stiff upper lip." Boys get big boy conditioning: "Big boys don't cry." Girls are given permission to cry, but then are labeled weak.

Yet feelings that are not experienced and expressed in a healthy manner continue to exist. They are maintained in organ systems and tissues of the body. Anxiety, for example, constricts muscles and blood flow and speeds up the heart rate. When people do not address their emotional lives effectively, important body parts and systems break down under accumulated stress. A physical symptom or an emotional crisis occurs when internal pressure exceeds the holding capacity. Nervous breakdowns, many industrial and auto accidents and most illnesses are the grand finales of such a process.

As I've said throughout this book, emotions from the past that are not cleared also interfere with present relationships; much of what you now feel is driven by childhood experiences. Thus, it is important to release these old and forgotten feelings in safe ways.

The release of painful emotions in such forms as crying, trembling, shouting, laughter and non-repetitive talking is the way in which human beings undo tensions and anxieties that hurtful experiences have placed upon us. For instance, heavy grief, which seems to be the deepest of emotional hurts, is released with tears and sobbing. Fear or terror is undone by shivering, teeth chattering and cold perspiration, sometimes accompanied by the urge to urinate or defecate. Anger is released through angry words, loud sounds, violent physical movements, tears and warm perspiration. Zest and joy are expressed somatically by smiles, laughter and an inner sense of well-being.

One kind of emotional release is as important as another and they all involve somatic processes. There is no need to fear releases when they are done safely. When the process is concluded, the mind clears and access to rational thought and the nurturing joyful spirit returns. It is important to know that you can decide when to release anger and how to do it safely.

Emotional release can be useful in the *Reflection* stage of the *Three R's*. Clearing strongly held feelings is best done with a caring, nonjudgmental listener. There is no need to fear a strong feeling or to act out this feeling. Simply let yourself feel it, express the somatic manifestations of that feeling and then deliver the information about the feeling safely.

Take long, slow breaths. This goes a long way toward getting through the process of release. Likewise, disciplines such as yoga, meditation and the martial arts, especially when practiced regularly, can assist awareness and the ability to feel and express such emotions.

Managing Fear

Threats, intimidation, uncertainty and lack of information are a few sources of fear. When these occur, fear always arises; it is a survival issue and therefore important not to ignore, deny or repress. Make fear your friend and learn what it has to teach.

There are two kinds of personal responses available whenever a fear is sensed. A *regressive* response is non-constructive and paralyzing. It is characterized by defensive withdrawal, fighting or fleeing, dependence or malicious obedience and has negative, destructive consequences. A *responsive* approach is constructive and productive. It is characterized by the use of the *Three R's*, active listening, attention to feelings and identification of the problem that needs to be solved. The responsive approach produces positive, rewarding results and builds trust.

When you are in the grip of fear, remember these cautions:
* Stay off the Drama Triangle
* Know your *inner family theater* and its players
* No lies, no secrets, no rescues, no power plays
* Remember that crisis is a time of both danger and opportunity—use it to grow personally and to accomplish new purposes

Managing Sadness and Grief

Grief serves to heal us from separation and loss. It is a natural response to a disappointment in life, whether large or small, and may last anywhere from a few moments to months or years. It is a way of helping restore ourselves upon learning of the death of a loved one, friend or pet; separation or divorce; loss of a job or a chronic or life-threatening illness in a loved one or ourselves. For most of us, such losses and disappointments are often fraught with anguish. It is important to acknowledge these events when they happen and provide time to process the emotional aspects connected with them. Remember, until the emotion is processed, rational thinking is diminished and sometimes even shut down.

Even though grief and sadness are natural, many of us do not understand what healthy grief is nor even how to grieve. We frequently suppress our grief because we're afraid of feeling the pain. We act grown up. We remember the parental injunctions "Big boys don't cry" or "We mustn't show our feelings." So we hold in our grief and never let it go, never complete it, no matter how light or heavy the grief may be.

If we do not express grief in a healthy way, it impacts us in unanticipated ways in our daily lives. When we stuff grief and it disappears inside us, we are in a constant state of unrecognized tension. We are said to be *frozen in grief*. We only partially feel our emotions, if at all. Sometimes we become obsessively preoccupied with our feelings of grief. Unexpressed and unprocessed grief will drain our energy and attention, erode productive work and diminish the joy and meaning in our lives.

Though you may not be aware of it, you do have a choice concerning grief and sadness. Deep grief must be allowed to run its natural course, but lighter grief can be processed and cleared in a few minutes or hours depending upon its intensity. A commitment to complete the grief process is required. You must also release any attachment to suffering, allowing the natural process of grief to proceed until it is completed. If you are conscious of the process, you can set it aside for a time and then come back to it and continue your expression until you feel finished with it and can return to your alert, aware, in-charge self.

There are three phases to the grief process: The first phase, shock and denial, has numbness and disbelief about it. The middle phase is suffering and disorganization. It contains anger, guilt, regrets, rationalizations, depression and bargaining with God. The third phase is acceptance and reorganization and features relief. You can move through these phases at a good pace or get stuck in one of them. To process grief you need empathic friends, tears—lots of tears—and permission to move through these stages with their accompanying somatic expressions. When you give yourself this permission, you allow the grief to pass.

Managing Joy and Care

Many homes are joyless. A home without meaning and joy is a dreary and cheerless place. It is all too often a place where fear and anger reside.

Joy is an expression of happiness. Much that is mistaken for joy is not truly authentic joy. Sometimes people feel that possessions bring happiness and so spend time and money accumulating unnecessary belongings. This behavior may conceal some degree of depression. Some people feel that doing something is happiness. Such activity can encompass hobbies such as knitting, golfing or gardening. When these activities provide a creative outlet, they produce genuine happiness; however, when done merely out of habit or competition, they can also have compulsive and unhealthy aspects to them. Some feel that power over others helps to obtain happiness. Some see partying as joyful, but sometimes there is an escapist quality about partying. Happiness is not escapist. Alcohol abuse, use of drugs and other addictions are ways of anesthetizing and avoiding emotional pain, not roads to happiness.

Happiness, like real love, is self-produced and flows from being self-contained. True happiness fills us with a sense of well-being and cannot be derived from a source outside of ourselves. Pain, conflict, loss, struggles and disappointments do not suddenly vanish. Happiness makes room for sadness. Happiness sometimes has peaks of joy, but these rise from a foundation of contentment. This contentment is anchored in an awareness of the beauty, harmony and wonder of life. Reasons for happiness, contentment and joy exist everywhere—in health, life, the mystery and marvels of nature and our own existence.

Happiness may be, as Robert A. Johnson says, as simple as "stirring oatmeal"—enjoying even the little pleasures and responsibilities that maintain our lives.

You can create a home wherein true happiness resides, using the following four tenets:

1. Home is a place where you feel you are doing something important and significant;
2. Home is a place where there are opportunities to grow and stretch your competence and talents;
3. Home is a place to create a sense of intimacy, mutual support and reciprocal love;
4. Home provides a sense of meaning and purpose to life.

Many aspects of these four facets of home life must be built and nurtured inside your home in a responsible way by both partners. Each of you must bring your own internal emotional resources to the fore and participate in the creation of a rewarding and happy home.

It is possible to posit the *Law of Family Well-being:*

The life of an effective family depends upon successfully processing the ongoing emotional life within it.

Now that you know how to manage feelings, you can understand how this law leads to two corollaries:

Corollary One: The only relationship that works is one on which we work.

Corollary Two: Maintaining passion and healthy sex depends upon conscious processing of the emotional aspects of the relationship.

Work in the absence of joy is empty and spawns despair; joy unsupported by work is decadent, soulless and lacking in fulfillment.

A partnership who learned this lesson well, Laura and Sean McChesney are the parents of two teenagers, Billy and Susan. Sean and Laura sought help during a Stage 3 crisis when unresolved childhood issues led Sean to withdraw from full participation in his marriage and family. He began to spend most of his time studying and practicing for his pilot's license, often missing dinner and weekend outings. Laura

*eventually confronted Sean with his absenteeism and he admit-
ted he was looking for the excitement he had missed in his
youth. His admission triggered all of Laura's own unresolved
issues. Since both had grown up in severely dysfunctional, abusive and neglectful families, both had strong fears, he of engulfment and she of abandonment. These fears kept them from
fully trusting each other, leading them to defeat the very intimacy and love they craved using the solutions they'd developed as children to cope: Sean withdrew in fear and anger and
Laura tried to be perfect to get his attention. The more she
tried, the more he withdrew, thus creating the very thing they
feared—the loss of affection.*

*Willingness and courage brought them to counseling and
they both worked hard to uncover the truth about their* inner
family theaters *and the childhood decisions that no longer
worked. They learned a better, more honest way of communicating and in time, joy, dedication and passion joined with the
already strong commitment and loyalty they felt. They were
then able to move successfully into Stage 4, where maturity
and intention create intentional love.*

*With their marriage stabilized, the McChesneys decided to
plan a family sabbatical to France and launched a family development program to help make it happen. It was during one of
these family development meetings that the turning point
came, leading the McChesney family into the full-fledged sta-
tus of Stage 5. Daughter Susan asked permission to give her
mother some constructive feedback and confessed, "Mom,
when you take over the tasks I've volunteered to take care of,
I feel like you're talking down to me, like you think I'm small
and incompetent." Laura struggled with her fear of criticism,
of not being perfect, and then she broke down in huge sobs.
Son Billy came out of his chair to put his arms around his
mother, in a reflection of the comfort she had provided many
times to him. When the air had cleared, the understanding
between mother and daughter was evident. In a subsequent*

family development meeting, Sean admitted he did not share his son's empathic response to Laura's tears, but felt cold and resistive instead. The facilitator reminded Sean that all his life he had been punished for having feelings; the message was that it was dangerous for him to express them. He suggested that Sean would not be able to feel Laura's pain until he was able to feel his own. At the close of the meeting, Sean received high praise for his dedication as a husband, father and provider... and for being a man who cares deeply but has a difficult time reaching those feelings. Tears filled Sean's eyes and his long repressed but genuine feelings finally came to the surface.

Susan had given her family a profound gift. In finding her "voice," she brought a vulnerability to the family that led to an acceptance of one another that had not been there before. Using the tools and techniques they have learned to communicate effectively, to appreciate and honor each other and to resolve conflict, the McChesneys are living the Law of Family Well-being. *This family became cohesive, resourceful, cooperative, joyful and nurturing.*

The *Marital Melodrama* Revisited

If you and your partner have done the work, you are now aware of your *inner family theaters*, the pitfalls of the Drama Triangle and the insidious nature of the *marital melodrama*. But the scenes and players of your childhoods are deeply ingrained and even your new-found awareness and commitment will not protect you from a repeat performance.

In *The Agony of It All*, Joy Davidson observed that most women are introduced to drama modalities in childhood as a means of generating excitement. She identified three styles of personal drama: The Drama of Conflict and Crisis, The Drama of Challenge and The Drama of Rebellion. Davidson explains that women:

> *...continually repeat the actions, extract the pleasure, and put up with the anguish relating to our personal drama—usually*

without recognizing its patterns or understanding why they occur. It isn't that we enjoy the agony of it all, but that we find satisfaction in drama's stimulation and may unconsciously believe that a trade off is necessary—a pound of excitement for an equal ration of hurt and confusion.

Davidson suggests these erroneous beliefs run many women. By uncovering the scenarios that rule their lives, women can learn to move forward and avoid the backlash of pain and the loss of intimacy that flows from their use.

It would be a self-deception on the part of men to think they don't play similar drama games. Male drama derives from and is anchored in aggressive and defensive postures. Men are frequently bound by anger, threats and rage; blocked by their inability to be vulnerable and gentle; locked into a *machismo* facade and power-oriented choices; trapped in power plays. The authentic male lies uneasily below the surface, hungry for love and attention, afraid to ask and denying the need. By uncovering the scenarios that rule their lives, men too can learn to move forward and avoid the backlash of pain and the loss of intimacy that arise from their use.

For both genders, the acceptance of personal responsibility leads the way off the dark stage of these and other dramas. Make a contract with yourself to:

- Learn and utilize information about your childhood;
- Learn which early childhood choices drive and detract from your self-development and interfere with your relationship;
- Gain more understanding about how you presently behave;
- Be ever more skillful at knowing what choices support emotional growth.

It is this inner journey that will lead you and your partner away from the *marital melodrama* and toward a committed, cooperative love that can only be attained as you and your partner come to know yourselves. Intentional, mature love does not promise happiness, but gives you the tools with which you may work to fashion relationships that are communicative, respectful, emotionally safe, satisfying and mutually enriching. To love your partner is a conscious choice you must make each day.

Even as learning more about yourself allows you to develop intentional love, the power of intentional love frees you to become more fully yourself. To love another does not require that you give up any part of yourself; rather it serves to enhance yourself.

Endeavor: Please Please Me

Overview
In this Endeavor, you will learn to give freely what your partner most wants from you and to receive graciously the gifts your partner has to offer. You will rediscover what pleases each of you. Then you'll learn to negotiate these so you can please each other in a regular, consistent and nurturing manner.

Activities
1. **Memories**
   a. In your personal notebook start a new page and title it *Things you do that make me feel loved and cared for*. Write down this sentence and complete it with as many different endings as you choose: "I feel loved and cared for when you..."
   b. Recall the romantic stage of your relationship and identify any caring behaviors you used to do for your partner that you are no longer doing. Using a separate page in your notebook titled *Things I loved about our courtship*, complete this sentence with as many different endings as you choose: "I felt loving and caring toward you when I..."

After completing these items, come together and share your lists.

2. **Hopes**
Respond to these items in your individual notebooks.
   a. Now think of some caring and loving behaviors you have always wanted but for which you never asked. These can be private fantasies or wishes. *This list should not include things under contention or conflict between you.* Those must be negotiated at another time.
   b. Title a page in your notebook *Things I hope for* and complete the following sentence as many times as you choose: "I hope you will do or say..." Before you come together to share your lists, prioritize the items in the order of their importance to you. Give each one a number, with 1 being the most important.

Now come back together and, each taking turns, share your prioritized list without interruption. Ask questions for clarification if needed. If there are any behaviors requested by your partner that you are not willing to do, it is important to tell your partner and eliminate them from the list.

3.   Honoring Your Partner

Beginning tomorrow, give your partner *two* caring behaviors each day. You will use your partner's list to make your selections, but you will each do the caring behaviors unasked. If you run out of choices after several days, simply repeat them. Acknowledge the receipt of each caring gift from your partner with a simple "thank you."

It is quite common to experience resistance with this exercise. Go against the resistance and keep doing the caring behaviors until you overcome it. Pay attention to your encouraging inner voices and tune out the judgmental or cynical voices. There is great positive power in the gifts you are giving. Allow yourself to experience the pleasure of receiving simple gifts from your partner.

Sharing the Process
- How do you feel about this Endeavor?
- Did you sense any resistance? How did you overcome it?
- Do you sense any return or increase of the feelings you had when your relationship was new?

Appreciations
- Share at least two appreciations that you felt for your partner during these activities.
- Share a special heartfelt feeling you have for your partner right now.

Close With—
- A plan for a special evening together.
- A warm, long hug.

Chapter 11

Inspiring Intimacy

A sincere heart can make a stone bloom.
Chinese Proverb

If love is an intentional choice and if **the only relationship that works is the one on which you and your partner work**, then what of romance? Must you really give up all notions of the sweet mystery, magic and excitement you have come to know and cherish as romance? The answer is yes—and no. For once you relinquish your old ideas about love and romance, they can be replaced with a new and richer kind of love—an ever present resource to be drawn upon—to carry you through the waxing and waning of the mundane, the misunderstandings, the daily-ness of your lives. With commitment and loyalty as the keys, you can ignite and inspire intimacy. Where love is a conscious, intentional choice you and your partner make every day, romance is the icing on the cake—sweeter and richer than you ever dreamed possible. How?

In chapter 1 you and your partner learned of the *Romantic Illusions* and the *Marital Realities* which help you to make the distinction between the romantic notions you must relinquish and a new kind of intimacy made possible through the work you have done. As you and your partner look again at the *Marital Realities*, you'll be heartened by how much you both have taken in and inspired by the progress you have made in the journey toward yourselves and each other.

Illusion #1 expressed a belief in the magic of enchantment—that romance would fuse you and your partner into soulmates who share all of your feelings and all of your dreams, thus making you whole and complete. Today you know that marriage provides the opportunity for wholeness, *if* you and your partner are willing to work at it.

Illusion #2 put forth the idea that romance will always flourish. It has been dispelled by the knowledge that marriages go through developmental stages and that even in good marriages, feelings of love wax and wane.

Illusion #3 suggested that if your mate really loved you, he or she would change for you. Now you have learned that you must respect the separate interests of your partner and that mature love allows and honors the differences.

Illusion #4 declared that your mate should just know what you feel, want and need. You have now gained new self-awareness that gives both of you the ability to ask honestly for what you need and want.

Illusion #5, the belief that passion and intensity must be constant and unchanging, has been dispelled. Now you know that the difficult times offer opportunities to grow through mutual respect and celebration of each other—that healthy marriages change and grow, keeping them vital and alive.

Illusion #6 demanded constant and continuous togetherness. Now you have learned not only to recognize the importance of your separate identities, but also to pay attention to a third presence, the relationship itself.

Illusion #7 taught each partner to be afraid of anger, conflict, arguing and fighting, and to believe these were signs that love has taken flight. Now you have been offered ways to work through these, assuring you that they are natural features of any relationship.

Illusion #8 purported that sexual interest is an accurate measure of love; however, by exploring your sensuality with your partner, you have debunked that idea. Instead, your partner and you can use the element of commitment to create a safe place to explore your sexual differences.

Illusion #9 explored the idea that your partner is to blame for the way you feel. You have now learned to take responsibility for your own feelings and to express yourselves with love and kindness.

Illusion #10, which extolled the belief that marriage should always be fair and equal, can be dispelled for good, because now you have learned to love without expectations and to give without keeping track.

By now you are aware that marriages built on these flimsy fabrics of illusion are doomed, while those that embrace the realities replacing them will flourish. The work you two have done so far has helped you to abandon the notion that to work on a marriage means love has failed. Remember your new mantra: **The only relationship that works is one on which we work.** In fact, those couples who do the work express their love in devoted and clearly unfailing terms.

You and your partner now are committed to working for a healthy, conscious, joyful marriage. You no longer expect your mate to satisfy your unmet childhood needs; instead you take responsibility for meeting your own needs, searching yourself for the inner creative strength to do so. You realize you are married to a real live human being, not a mythical soulmate, so you value your partner's uniqueness and are willing to help him or her meet his or her needs. Thoughtful intention now helps you to manage impulses. You are learning to talk with your partner kindly, thoughtfully and respectfully and to negotiate in a fair and considerate manner. In this way you can communicate hopes and wishes to your partner, for you do not expect him or her to meet hidden or unexpressed ones. Together, you and your partner will see the relationship through the joys, the angers, the fears and the sorrows, knowing that these form the foundation of a rewarding human connection.

With your new-found knowledge, awareness and skills you can now begin to build the relationship you've always wanted—the one you've always deserved. You and your partner who have come this far already are feeling the rewards of the conscious marriage, a real relationship far beyond romance. Though you've both come a great way, the work isn't over yet. Here, in the comfort and safety of your no-exit marriage or relationship, you can cultivate freedom, joy and intimacy. Start with intimacy.

The Search for Intimacy

In adolescence, everyone encounters the struggle to find and establish a unique identity. The puzzle of your teen years required you to settle upon a personal identity forged from unconscious childhood choices and conscious efforts to be what you would like to be and do what you would choose to do. Sometimes the identity you developed was driven by powerful peer pressure which occluded the real you deep inside. Some adolescents even have to create another false self, as they did when they were toddlers, this time to survive in the land of peers. Every time a person creates a false identity, she or he pushes the real one down. A person's true self may be so hidden from view that he or she no longer knows or recognizes that part of him- or herself.

Even before this identity struggle of your teenage years was complete, you were plunged into the paradoxical problem of isolation versus intimacy. This struggle for intimacy, which characterizes the transition from boy to man and girl to woman, is a difficult one. It presents a crisis we all encounter in early adulthood.

When you choose a partner with whom to mate, you create the reality of a relationship. Making the choice takes two *yes*es—one *yes* from each partner—but implies a million *no*es. These two *yes*es may be more or less intentional but, as we have seen, they are usually driven from unconscious needs to which both partners are blind. So long as the *yes* is never said, so long as the commitment remains unspoken, the possibility for intentional love remains only a possibility. This is what happened with Peter and Rebecca, the couple discussed early in this book whose attraction as young co-workers was rekindled at midlife, only to end abruptly when reality shattered the illusion of their romance.

> *Their come-together, break-apart dance ended at the*
> *fourth breakup. Neither one, in the end, could bring him- or*

herself to say a loud and resounding "yes" to the risk of making a full commitment to each other—largely for reasons of unchanged childhood decisions, unrealistic expectations and the projection of painful emotional material onto the other. While Rebecca was willing to explore herself and face the changes she would need to make in order to become a more loving partner, she found herself doing the work alone. It is a possibility that even with Peter's cooperation, there were not enough of the other four elements—friendship, compatibility, affection and sensuality—to sustain them. However, because Peter was unwilling to look beyond the surface of his feelings, he and Rebecca were never able to find out. As of this writing, they are both alone... perhaps still wondering why.

When the risk of saying yes is never taken, identity is left unconfirmed, intimacy is lost and a life well lived is traded for a bitter harvest of alienation, isolation, stagnation and despair. Choosing to say yes, the committed partnership begins and the first few steps toward intimacy are taken.

Bridging the Gulf between Intimacy and Isolation

Accepting responsibility for your own life may feel isolating. Responsibility means that you have stopped blaming another or others for your mistakes and hold no one but yourself accountable for your own comfort and protection. Because of this, facing yourself and confronting your life may bring about feelings of panic, desperation, anguish and fear. In this moment you must become your own best friend. You must become the nurturing parent to your own unloved inner child. In this process you will find self-discovery, self-forgiveness and self-knowledge.

When you risk enough to know yourself, you can un-self-consciously extend the love you find inside to others. This is intimacy. If you wish to be yourself, you must be willing to reveal yourself. Isolation and intimacy are part and parcel of each other, for to love fully, you must know and love yourself and this requires the loneliness of responsibility and self-examination. Love is the bridge between intimacy and isolation.

Wholeness and Forgiveness

A discussion of intimacy would be incomplete without mention of forgiveness. Forgiveness can only be truly accessed when both partners have achieved wholeness and can hold and tolerate two emotionally contradictory images of each other—one in which your partner is seen as frustrating or hurtful, the other in which your partner is seen as valuable and loved. The realization that both of you are made up of both good and bad aspects indicates awareness of your wholeness.

Henry Wilmer observed that in time, everything evolves into its opposite: shadow to consciousness, consciousness to shadow, hero to heel, heel to hero, light to dark, dark to light. The word *enantiodromia* means running contrariwise—everything turning into its opposite. Intimately connected with this concept is the notion that our greatest strengths house our greatest weaknesses and our greatest weaknesses house our greatest strengths. Thus we must learn to accept both parts of ourselves, for these opposites are essential and intimate parts of each other. It is this tension that is so integral to who we are and what we become. If you are blind to it, it will surprise and overwhelm you.

When you and your mate become aware that each of you has both good and bad parts, sadness will emerge. Such sadness is important, because it signals that the grandness of self is receding into the realm of fiction and dreams. It is then that forgiveness, empathy and compassion are possible. Salvation through the marriage no longer beckons, but damnation no longer threatens. Knowledge of both good and bad together does result in the loss of paradise, but with that loss comes the chance for an intentionally loving, chosen relationship.

Bruce and Nancy, of whom I spoke earlier, are the couple whose perfect marriage disintegrated through unmet and unrealistic expectations and turned into a nasty divorce. Resentment, retaliation and rage reigned until diligent work in counseling reunited them in a second marriage.

Bruce and Nancy remarried four years after their tumultuous divorce. They had discovered their mutual willingness to take the risk and to engage fully in the commitment and work they knew it would take to sustain a lasting relationship. Fifteen years later, their son is now in his mid-teens. He is already showing great depth, maturity and self-confidence—the clear result of having grown up in an emotionally literate home. Bruce continues to participate in a men's support group that he founded in order to stay connected to his feelings and stay conscious of the tools he needs to use to maintain and nurture his connection to his partner, Nancy. They both work hard to maintain their emotional literacy and self-awareness. "Fifteen years later, the most important keys to our marriage," says Bruce, "are the ability to understand our own inner family theaters, the ability to feel remorse and the willingness to ask for and give forgiveness." Both Nancy and Bruce have acquired the authenticity and humility required to unlock those key elements. The reward is a loving, satisfying and nurturing marriage far beyond their imaginings.

Joy and Freedom

There are those who seek in love and marriage only a safe harbor from a world of hostility and fear. They wish to gratify their own emotional needs. Blindly, they proceed without giving thought to the meaning of commitment. This is usually an illusory pursuit, for love without commitment is bound to fade. The relationship becomes only a way to avoid the risks of self-discovery and transformation. Under such circumstances love and marriage are both certain to wither and die.

Real romance is kindled and nurtured, erupting at times into warm and passionate flames and kept alive by commitment, loyalty and devotion to the other. When you engage in a fully conscious marriage and make the choice every day to love and attend to each other, then romance can restore, recharge and revitalize your love.

In the end and throughout the duration of the marriage, you and your partner must be conscious of your power to create and destroy.

Only by being conscious and aware and taking responsibility for your own emotional needs can you have the joy and freedom you seek. By giving up what you need and giving to your partner instead, you will receive many times over what you were after all along. You will arrive at freedom by committing to each other. The joy is in the daily comfort and freedom found in conscious marriages—freedom to discover and become more fully yourselves.

The process of self-transformation occurs within the context of groups and relationships—a result of the interplay between self and world. The choice to love one among the wonderful many is a life-altering and defining one. You are challenged to learn about yourself, to become yourself and to create an unknown possibility by encountering another. In "Dream Weavers," the Endeavor that follows this chapter, you will create that unknown possibility when you describe your dream relationship to each other and together decide how to make it come true.

Endeavor: Dream Weavers

Overview

In earlier Endeavors, you and your mate have examined the romantic beginnings of your marriage and looked clearly into each other's eyes, discovering your hidden assumptions and expectations. You have reviewed the realities and illusions of your marriage. In addition, you have revisited the past, connecting it to where you and your partner find yourselves today. You have decided to welcome marriage's warm embrace. You have discovered the *inner family theaters* and your *marital melodrama*, which contributed to earlier conflict. You have learned how to communicate effectively and to release power in favor of love. You have cultivated the joys of "stirring oatmeal" together and the strength of mature, intentional love.

Genuine intimacy is within your grasp. In this Endeavor you will explore your feelings about your marriage in a letter to your partner. You have learned to communicate safely. Now each of you can consciously create your dream and then create a mutual dream for your lives together.

Remember in this Endeavor to give your partner your full attention. Listen without comment, without interruption and with loving kindness. Look directly into your partner's eyes and simply listen. Resist any temptation to defend, explain, attack or blame. If you feel the need to defend, attack or shift the blame away from yourself, you are not taking responsibility for your feelings and actions. Remember that you are creating a mutual dream for your marriage.

Activities

1. **Creating Your Dream**
   a. As a couple find a safe, secluded spot where you can be alone and uninterrupted; perhaps take a picnic to a favorite place. Take as much time apart as you need to each write a paragraph or two in your individual notebooks about your ideal dream for the relationship. Then come together and read your dreams

to each other. Remember—no comments, no judgments or interruptions.

b.   Now create your mutual dream. Write this down in your notebooks or choose one of you to be the note taker.
 1.   Identify and create a dream you both share.
 2.   Identify some specific goals which will help bring the dream into reality.
 3.   Identify several specific steps you will each take as individuals and several steps you will take together to help bring the dream into reality.

2.   What is it like being married to me?

Take some time separately to write a letter to your partner, in your individual notebook, answer this question as if your partner had asked you, "What is it like being married to me?" Make your letter authentic, as full of meaning and as focused on specifics as you can. This is a letter to the one you love, so it's okay to show your feelings. Tell the truth yet be considerate, polite and kind.

When you are finished, come together and read your letters to each other. Simply listen. Resist any temptation to defend, explain, attack or blame.

Sharing the Process:
 •   Did you share honestly and without reservations?
 •   Were there any surprises?
 •   Did you use your Guidelines for Safe Communication?
 •   Is there anything you would like your partner to clear up?
 •   What was most important as you shared your dreams and your letters?

Appreciations

Again, remember to use eye contact and to listen carefully.

- Share one or two focused behaviors or feelings that you appreciate about your partner that flowed from listening to his or her letter.
- Share one way your partner's dream was meaningful to you.

Close With—

- An authentic "I love you" and long, warm hug.

Chapter 12

Reaching the Pinnacle

Love is an endless act of forgiveness,
a tender look which becomes a habit.
Peter Ustinov

Mature love is the predominant creative force we know. When two people form a relationship through the exercise of conscious choice and intention, they bring a formidable power together.

Each of your choices brings you closer to wisdom or to despair. To choose greatly, you must be self-aware. You have learned that in order to be self-aware, you must dispatch illusory romance, transcend your *script*-driven choices and work to create a passionate, loving relationship. These are not easy tasks. They take work, but it is work that has the fullness of the human spirit as company. In this, the final chapter of our journey together, let us look with gratitude and love upon the rewards of that work.

M. Scott Peck, author of several books including *The Road Less Traveled,* once commented that when he and his wife quit trying to change each other and accepted one another for who they were, their marriage began to work. This is the starting point for true cooperation and eventual harmony.

Cooperation is essential to mature love. "Cooperative love asks that neither the head nor the heart be neglected even when their demands are conflicting," writes Jane Goldberg. Continuing, she writes:

> *Cooperative love is a love that is a promise of what is new and different within ourselves. It doesn't promise happiness, but it gives us the tools with which we may work to fashion relationships that are communicative, respectful, emotionally satisfying, and mutually enriching.*

You and your mate must truly know yourselves and must also have the ability to decode and translate each other's communications. With these two skills, true cooperation can begin within the partnership and the creation of harmony becomes possible. True harmony is obtainable when both of you

- are willing to process your emotions in a responsible, constructive and loving way;
- use effective negotiation skills;
- create and share a dream for yourselves as a couple, then take responsibility for the dream.

The good news is that, if you have done the work suggested in the previous eleven chapters, the willingness, the skills and the creation of shared dreams are already working for you, leading you toward a pinnacle far beyond the illusions of the transitory romance with which you began. Released from the tethers of your childhoods, no longer ruled by your *inner family theaters*, you can find great freedom in loving each other. Contained within the freedom of loving are the priceless gifts of intimacy, empowerment, passion and respect. We have seen that for Bruce and Nancy, Karen and Jim, Mark and Mary, David and Shelley and the McChesneys, those gifts were realized. For Gwen and Lance, however, the jury is still out. This is our love-at-first-sight nurse and businessman whose childhood *scripts* drove Gwen to be too critical and Lance to be overly sensitive.

When last we discussed them (in chapter 8), Lance was still "punishing" Gwen for being overly demanding. He had not yet realized that he was projecting his feelings about his hyper-critical, punishing mother onto Gwen. And Gwen had not yet realized that she was projecting her fear of her neglectful, alcoholic father onto Lance. Through hard work and empathic guidance from a skilled counselor, this couple learned to recognize the actors from their inner family theaters *and the behaviors in each other that triggered them. They used their Guidelines for Fair Fighting each time an argument began, doling out equal measures of commitment and forgiveness. They now had the tools and the understanding needed to move into the heroic period of their marriage—to build a home, have a family and put meaning into their lives.*

Gwen became pregnant and in her eighth month, she was diagnosed with a syndrome that put the baby's life at risk and seriously jeopardized her own health. A decision was made to induce labor and she delivered a healthy baby girl. Gwen, however, was still in danger. Over the following week, all the old marital melodramas were swept away. Lance was at her side in every way—physically present, emotionally supportive, intentionally devoted and dedicated. Gwen and Lance laughed together, cried together, were afraid together. In place of the old behaviors, there arose a deeply felt and shared love that neither had experienced before. Within the context of this bonding event, Gwen let go of her "demands" on Lance; she could see he was not her neglectful, alcoholic father. Lance let go of his fear that he would be lost in Gwen's demands and needs; he could see that she was not his critical, punishing mother. They both surrendered completely to the warm embrace of their marriage. The lessons they had worked so hard to learn now came effortlessly, for they finally understood the power of intentional love.

Marriage, supported by intentional love and conscious commitment, embraces the promise of continual unfolding. Love and marriage are not the ultimate solution to problems, but a sustained striving for completeness. The dynamics within a coupled relationship are a constant striving for transformation, wholeness and goodness. To turn away from love and marriage is to choose death among the living. Real life is full of risks and promise, of fear, anger, joy and sadness. A committed marriage provides the safe and loving harbor wherein you can feel and express the full range of those feelings and come to honor them, yourself and your partner.

Once the illusion of romance is slain, it is replaced through intention and choice by a deeply felt bond. This bond sustains the struggle for mutual understanding and respect. In addition to spawning affection and contentment between partners, it nourishes a persevering commitment to know yourself and your partner; it encourages sensual harmony and fosters attachment and responsiveness. This, in turn, generates and enriches a mature love. And when mature love is present, life takes on meaning and purpose.

It is important here to reintroduce Georgia, the heroic female half of a couple we met in chapter 6—a couple who was not able to cultivate mature love. This is the out-of-work artist and successful caterer whose twenty-year marriage ended in divorce.

> *Georgia and Tom were never able to transition successfully out of the disintegration of Stage 3. After their divorce each was left to sort through what went wrong on his or her own. Tom continued through his middle age to attack, blame and defend—even after the divorce, remaining loyal to the pain of his childhood. He was stuck in the grief, anger and hurt generated by the early contradiction of his father's demands versus his own dreams. Georgia, on the other hand, made great strides in self-awareness, overcoming the voices of her* inner family theater *and building a strength she never knew she had. In a letter to her counselor, years after the divorce, she wrote: "I am learning so many things. How to stand by myself*

and to set boundaries very clearly so that no one can violate them. It feels great, part of becoming my own woman, independent, autonomous and free. Perhaps I will one day find a relationship with a man who is sensitive and mature enough to build a strong and loving life together—a life that will show my children that not all marriages are doomed to failure." Georgia has emerged from the pain of her childhood and the divorce from Tom with a consciousness that gives her freedom, strength and joy.

The struggle to create an enriched, cooperative relationship depends upon balancing what Robert A. Johnson, in *Ecstasy: Understanding the Psychology of Joy*, identifies as "the morality of romance" with "the morality of commitment." The morality of commitment comes from the external world; the social order—indeed the very future of human existence—requires people to honor commitment. The morality of romance is the truth hidden in individual souls. Romance should be encouraged and allowed to unfold inwardly. As we have seen, when the imagined quality of romance is allowed to dominate external lives, it wreaks havoc and pain. But when each of these is honored—the need for commitment and the need for romance—they will no longer clash and compete but will bring peace and fulfillment in the world and in your dreams. In *Courage My Love: A Book to Light an Honest Path*, Merle Shain writes about the essence of commitment:

> *Commitment doesn't just mean to stay with someone through thick and thin. It means to make something work, and to help it keep on working, so each of you can trust yourself to the other in that private place, knowing that the other will do what has to be done, whatever that something is. And knowing that you always have the spiritual margin to get derailed again, and yet still grow old together with everything intact.*

Good relationships, including good marriages, are intentional and chosen. There are no perfect couples; there are enduring couples.

People who select each other—whether for love or other reasons—remain vibrant and alive in their relationship because they choose to do so. Their love is deep and mature. They are friends. They are compatible. They are affectionate. They are committed. They have a healthy respect for themselves, their partners and the needs and dreams of each. They negotiate their differences with grace while allowing and encouraging the full development of the other. They have created, negotiated and renegotiated an emotional contract with agreed-upon understandings and guidelines based on respect and trust. In so doing, they have honored themselves and each other.

We met Karen and Jim, a couple in their middle years, in chapter 4. If you recall, Karen lost her voice and Jim couldn't hear. When we last saw them, they were bickering over a new print Karen had bought and the housework with which Jim never helps.

> *These two brought strong commitment and willingness to their counseling sessions. The foundation of their marriage rested on genuine friendship and a heartfelt love for each other. Over time, however, Jim's inattentiveness and Karen's weariness at having to "make" the marriage successful had worn her down. She admitted that her heart had turned to stone. In the work that followed, they quickly saw how the* scripts *from their childhoods had driven them each to behave in ways that triggered the other. Karen found her voice and began to ask for (rather than expect) the help she needed. Jim learned to listen (rather than ignore or tease) and discovered how easy it was to please her. They began to take responsibility for their own emotional material and strove hard to be clear, honest and forgiving. Today, Jim and Karen share a committed, mature and intentional love between them. This love is based on a thriving friendship, new-found understanding about each other and themselves, renewed compatibility and affection and genuine passion. As they reached the last of their counseling sessions, they decided to take a trip to the British Isles, a lifelong dream come*

*true for both. Within the safe harbor of a committed marriage,
Jim's sincere heart did indeed make Karen's stone heart bloom.*

When you support the one you love; when you put in the effort to know yourself well enough that you release your partner from the need to take care of you; when you take responsibility for meeting your own emotional needs; when you receive the love of your partner unconditionally and with grace; when you are able to give love without expectations or demands; then you honor yourself and your partner. Thus you can live in each moment a zestful, joyful, meaningful, rewarding life.

In the final Endeavor, "Looking Forward," you and your partner will create a vision for the future of your marriage and plan the steps needed to move toward it. Active and consequential love creates a closeness that nurtures the human spirit. This mature love engenders the intimacy that shapes society, forms the milieu in which children are reared and determines the outcome of the next generation. Having read this book and completed the Endeavors, you and your partner will contribute to that future—a better, more loving, more conscious world.

It is to you that I dedicate this original verse, "The Promise of True Love."

The Promise of True Love

*When mature love is absent
        romance turns bitter,
        discontent and hatred are spawned,
        drift and despair loom,
        cynicism and greed rule;
        the gentle, the vulnerable, and the weak
        are abandoned and scorned,
        the world becomes bleak and cruel.*

*Tyranny, fear and desolation are unleashed
        to prowl the planet,*

demeaning and diminishing the human spirit;
children are reared without love's presence,
sowing a whirlwind
that becomes a holocaust.

Love's challenge —
to create balance and consonance
between partners who have chosen
one another.

Romance, the illusion, the impostor, slain
by intention, deceit, or neglect, may
by deliberate choice, reawaken
from the ashes, arise
reborn and authentic,
powerful, passionate, and
fashion a profound connection,
creating a renewed, vital bond,
emancipated from the shadows,
ardent, robust, alive!

Energy, revitalized, courses between
the renewed, devoted lovers, and
sustains the struggle,
encourages mutual understanding,
supplies renewed respect,
spawns a deeper affection,
promotes passion and harmony, and
fosters attachment and responsiveness.

A mature love
nourishes a persevering commitment
to know myself and know my partner,
to give without qualms,
to struggle in love anew that

enriches intimacy,
engenders affection,
promotes active, consequential caring,
creates a poignant closeness,
nurtures the human spirit, and
gives life renewed meaning and purpose.

Intimacy's qualities shape society,
delineate the milieu of our children's lives,
determine the outcome of the next generation;
govern the style and mode of how our children choose
to share and take power from us; and this,
as history teaches us,
defines the quality of our lives, forecasts the future, and
makes possible a loving and peaceful world.

Robert H. Simmons

Endeavor: Looking Forward

Overview

You and your partner may now design your future with aware, loving and conscientious attention. In the Endeavor in chapter 11, you created your shared dream. Now you both will develop the necessary goals, strategies and steps to make that dream come true. Setting goals is taking your dream seriously. It is taking the vision of your future and giving it the mature loving energy you both now have for your marriage, plus the guidance needed to create that vision. The first step rests on the assumption that key aspects of your future can be designed and influenced by actions that can be taken now.

Activities

1. **Setting Goals**
   a. You and your partner should review your dream from the Endeavor in chapter 11. Think about what you want your lives to look like five, ten, twenty, thirty years from now. Consider your personal needs and desires, your children's needs, financial goals, recreational, spiritual and health matters. Reach for the stars but be realistic about what you can accomplish. Take some time to complete these sentences separately in your notebooks. Then reconvene and share your answers.
      1. To help us reach our dream together, my personal goals are...
      2. My ideas of how to reach our dream together are...
      3. I will take the following steps...
      4. I would like you to take the following steps...
      5. As a couple I would like us to take the following steps...

   b. When you have shared your answers with each other, identify the ones you agree on and develop for each a plan and a timeline. List the goals first. Under each one, write down the steps you will need to take to achieve it, plus a target date for when the goal will be accomplished. You will also identify which steps are his, which are hers and which will be shared. Here is an example of goal setting:

Goal Setting Example

GOAL		DATE
Goal #1:	Take a three-week trip to Italy	April of next year
His steps:	Research passport process	By next month
	Research air fares and hotels	By two months from now
Her steps:	Arrange house and pet sitters	By two months before departure
	Decide what to pack (cameras, travel books, clothing, etc.)	By one month before departure
Our steps:	Learn Italian	Beginning now
	Decide what we'll see and do	Six months ahead

GOAL		DATE
Goal #2:	To lose weight and establish a healthier lifestyle	Next month
His steps:	Check into gyms, health clubs, walking and running trials	By Monday
Her steps:	Research nutrition and healthy diet books	By Monday
Our steps:	Decide on an eating plan we can share	By Wednesday
	Agree on an exercise plan for both of us	By Wednesday

2. **The Intentional Love Letter**
   a. In a letter to your partner, share what you felt as you went through this book together, what you learned, how this improved or changed your relationship. What was the most valuable part for you? What do you plan to do differently?

What parts of this book helped you restore and enrich the love you seek? What has been the most significant change you have seen in your partner?

b.   Set the scene, make it warm, receptive and comfortable and in a relaxed way share your letters with each other.

Sharing the Process
- Is there a different feel to your relationship?
- Are you a more effective and active listener?
- What other realizations have you come to about being together?
- Have you noticed any differences about being together and talking to each other?
- What changes have you noticed in your marriage?

Appreciations
- Share two ways you feel your partner has changed and gained.
- Tell two ways you were affected by your experience with this book.

Before You End This Book...
- Make regular dates with each other where you will review what you have learned, clear what needs to be cleared and renew your commitment to each other.
- Decide how you will each take responsibility for doing that.
- Celebrate one another in small and simple ways.
- Renew your marriage from time to time by choosing a chapter from this book to review and redo the Endeavors.

Close With—
- A long, warm embrace and a deeply felt "I love you."
- Set a date for a dinner or a weekend away where you can celebrate the work you have done and the beginning of your new life together.

Bravo and brava to you and your partner, who have been courageous enough to have joined me in this voyage toward yourselves and
each other. In your new-found strength, vulnerability, self-knowledge
and willingness, you have transcended the dark deceits of *romance* and
emerged into the light of *true love*.

Glossary

Developmental Stages
Every couple goes through a developmental process involving successive stages. The progression to the next is based upon the successful negotiation of the preceding stage. When each preceding stage is successfully negotiated, a new challenge arises for which the past is prelude. More importantly, each preceding stage provides the resources people use to negotiate the next stage. A couple cannot evade, avoid or skip over a developmental stage.

Drama Triangle
The Drama Triangle is a convenient way to see how the scenes of your *marital melodrama* play out in your everyday life. There are three positions on the Drama Triangle—Rescuer, Victim, Persecutor. Action around the Drama Triangle is *script*-driven and is played for negative or positive acknowledgments.

Emotional Literacy

A state of awareness wherein you are alert to all of your feelings, how they are contained within and how they are expressed. It means developing a highly conscious knowledge of the link between your emotional life and your behavior.

Enmeshment

A condition wherein one partner surrenders to the dominance of the other, swallowing all contrary and problematic feelings.

Fear of Abandonment

Fear on the part of one partner that he or she will be left. This partner is needy and feels unworthy, undeserving of love. He or she is willing to do anything for the other partner in order to feel connected and avoid the terror of being alone.

Fear of Engulfment

Fear on the part of one partner of losing him- or herself to the domination of the other. This partner feels special and then insulted or outraged when that specialness is not recognized and acknowledged. This partner worries that his or her freedom is threatened.

Hostile-Dependence

A condition wherein a couple sinks into a pattern of antagonism followed by some form of tolerable dependence while awaiting an opportunity to renew the hostilities.

Inner Family Theater

The environment, the characters and the *scripts* created in childhood. The choices we made as children in response to our parents, siblings and others who affected us create the plots we incorporate into our lives as adults. For most, this theater is hidden from consciousness. The drama unfolds and the characters act with our partners as unwitting participants.

Law of Family Well-being
The life of an effective family depends upon successfully processing the ongoing emotional life within it.

Marital Melodrama
Any scene in a marriage or partnership that involves an interlocking system of needs, pain, rage and self-sacrifice. The scenes erupt, escalate and recede while the partners lie in wait to even the score. These *script*-driven scenes link the two partners in a seemingly endless succession of choreographed transactions that disclose a psychological arrangement between them.

Marital Realities
Characterize the underpinnings of a healthy marriage and must be understood by each partner in order to develop a conscious, emotionally literate and successful marriage.

Principle of Intentional Love
Mature and devoted love is an intentional decision, a conscious and daily choice that, through the practice of respect, responsibility and humility, can transcend the illusion of romance and transform relationships.

Projection
The act of splitting off a disowned and unwanted part of oneself, attributing it to someone else and then reacting to that part as separate from oneself.

Romantic Illusions
Erroneous thinking about love and relationships that ultimately lead to disappointment, disillusionment, discontent and loss.

Script
A set of unconscious inner guidelines that people create to survive emotionally in their childhoods. The *script* is an ongoing life plan that is taught behaviorally and reinforced throughout life. It drives people blindly until they understand it and take action to change it.

Soulmate
The illusion of the soulmate is a childlike hope that one partner will be exactly as the other envisioned. This becomes a setup for ultimate disappointment in mates and marriage, for no human can bear the weight of such hope and perfection.

The Three R's
A practice for managing emotional response in three steps: Receive—observe, listen to and see a stimulus. Reflect—instead of acting out immediately, assess and understand feelings first. Respond—act.

Transitional Crisis
A significant event or turning point in a developmental stage. The crisis is a time of both danger and opportunity. The danger is that if it is not resolved constructively, it will lead to a regressive alternative or contribute to the stagnation or demise of the relationship. The opportunity is to proceed to the next stage.

Bibliography

Adler, Warren. *War of the Roses*. Wyoming: Stonehouse Press, 1981.

Bader, Ellyn and Peter T. Pearson. *In Quest of the Mythical Mate: A Developmental Approach to Diagnosis and Treatment in Couples Therapy*. New York: Brunner/Mazel, Inc., 1988.

Berne, Eric. *Games People Play: The Psychology of Human Relationships*. New York: Grove Press, 1964.

Bion, Wilfred. *Experiences in Groups and Other Papers*. New York: Basic Books, 1961.

Campbell, Susan. *The Couple's Journey: Intimacy as a Path to Wholeness*. San Luis Obispo, California: Impact Publishers, 1980.

Davidson, Joy. *The Agony of It All: The Drive for Drama and Excitement in Women's Lives*. Los Angeles: Jeremy P. Tarcher, Inc. 1988.

Erikson, Erik H. *Childhood and Society*, 35th Anniversary Edition. New York: W. W. Norton & Company, 1950, 1963, 1985. Erickson's Eight Stages of Man have been summarized for purposes appropriate to this book.

_____. *Identity and the Life Cycle*. New York: W. W. Norton & Co., Inc., 1980.

_____. *Identity: Youth and Crisis*. New York: W. W. Norton & Co., Inc., 1968.

_____. *The Life Cycle Completed*. New York: W. W. Norton & Company, 1982.

Fromm, Erich. *Anatomy of Human Destructiveness*. New York: Holt, Rinehart and Winston, 1973.

_____. *The Art of Loving*. New York: Harper & Row, Publishers, 1956.

Goldberg, Jane G. *The Dark Side of Love: The Positive Role of Negative Feelings – Anger, Jealousy, Hate*. New Brunswick, N.J.: Transaction Publishers, 1999. Originally published in 1993 by G.P. Putnam's Sons.

Hajcak, Frank and Patricia Garwood. *Hidden Bedroom Partners: Needs and Motives That Destroy Sexual Pleasure*. San Diego, California: Libra Publishers, Inc. 1987.

Johnson, Robert A. *Ecstasy: Understanding the Psychology of Joy*. San Francisco: Harper & Row Publishers, Inc., 1987.

_____. *Femininity Lost and Regained*. New York: Harper & Row, Publishers, 1988.

_____. *He: Understanding Masculine Psychology*. New York: Harper & Row, Publishers, 1974.

_____. *Owning Your Own Shadow: Understanding the Dark Side of the Psyche*. San Francisco: HarperCollins, 1991.

_____. *She: Understanding Feminine Psychology*. New York: Harper & Row, Publishers, 1977.

_____. *We: Understanding the Psychology of Romantic Love*. New York: Harper & Row, Publishers, 1983.

Keen, Sam. *Fire in the Belly: On Being a Man*. New York: Bantam, 1991.

Lachkar, Joan. *The Narcissistic / Borderline Couple: A Psychoanalytic Perspective on Marital Treatment*. New York: Brunner/Mazel, 1992. Borderline Personality is referred to in this book as fear of abandonment; Narcissistic Personality is what I have called fear of engulfment for the purpose of demystifying the language and making these concepts accessible to couples committed to addressing and resolving their issues.

Lindbergh, Anne Morrow. *Gift From the Sea*. New York: Pantheon Paperback Edition, 1997.

Moore, Thomas. *Soul Mates: Honoring the Mysteries of Love and Relationship*. New York: HarperCollins, 1994.

Peck, Scott M. *The Road Less Traveled: A New Psychology of Love, Traditional Values and Spiritual Growth*. New York: Simon and Schuster, 1978.

Sashkin, Marshall. *Dealing With Feelings: Interpretive Guide*. Bryn Mawr, Pennsylvania: Organization Design and Development, Inc., 1987.

Shain, Merle. *Courage My Love: A Book to Light an Honest Path*. New York: Bantam Books, 1989.

_____. *Hearts That We Broke Long Ago*. New York: Bantam Books, 1983.

_____. *Some Men are More Perfect Than Others*. Philadelphia: J.B. Lippincott Company, 1973.

Sills, Judith. *A Fine Romance*. Los Angeles: Jeremy P. Tarcher, 1987.

_____. *How to Stop Looking for Someone Perfect and Find Someone to Love*. New York: St. Martin's Press, 1984.

Steiner, Claude. *Scripts People Live: Transactional Analysis of Life Scripts*. New York: Grove Press, 1974.

_____. *When a Man Loves a Woman: Sexual and Emotional Literacy for the Modern Man*. New York: Grove Press, 1988.

Wilmer, Harry A. *Practical Jung: Nuts and Bolts of Jungian Psychotherapy*. Wilmett, Illinois, Chiron Publications, 1987.

Suggested Readings

Andrews, Frank. *The Art and Practice of Loving*. New York: G.P. Putnam's Sons. 1991.

Bloomfield, Harold H., Sirah Vettese and Robert Kory. *Lifemates: The Love Fitness Program for a Lasting Relationship*. New York: New American Library, 1989.

Bly, Robert. *Iron John, A Book About Men*. New York: Addison-Wesley Publishing Co., Inc., 1990.

Bolen, Jean Shinoda. *Goddesses in Everywoman: A New Psychology of Women*. New York: Harper & Row, Publishers, Inc., 1984.

_____. *Gods in Everyman Reissue: Archetypes That Shape Men's Lives*. New York: Harper & Row, Publishers, Inc., 1989.

Borysenko, Joan. *Guilt is the Teacher, Love is the Lesson*. New York: Warner Books, 1990.

_____. *A Woman's Book of Life, The Biology, Psychology, and Spirituality of the Feminine Life Cycle.* New York: Riverhead Books, a division of G.P. Putnam, 1996.

_____. *A Woman's Journey to God.* New York: Riverhead Books, a division of G.P. Putnam, 1999.

Campbell, Susan. *Beyond the Power Struggle,* San Luis Obispo, California: Impact Publishers, 1984.

Carter, Steven and Julia Sokol. *He's Scared, She's Scared: Understanding the Hidden Fears that Sabotage Your Relationship.* New York: Dell Publishing, 1995.

Chapman, Gary. *The Five Love Languages: How to Express Heartfelt Commitment to Your Mate.* Chicago: Northfield Publishing, 1992, 1995.

Coleman, Paul W. *The Forgiving Marriage.* Chicago: Contemporary Books, 1989.

Creighton, James L. *Don't Go Away Mad.* N.Y. Doubleday, 1990.

DeAngelis, Barbara. *How to Make Love All the Time.* New York: Rawson Associates, 1987.

Delis, Dean C. with Cassandra Phillips. *The Passion Paradox: Patterns of Love and Power in Intimate Relationships.* New York: Bantam Books, 1990.

Diamond, Jed. *Looking for Love in All the Wrong Places: Overcoming Romantic and Sexual Addictions.* New York: G. P. Putnam's Sons, Inc., 1988.

Funt, Marilyn. *Grounds for Marriage.* New York: Dodd, Mead & Co., 1988.

Gabbard, Glen O. and Roy W. Menninger, Editors. *Medical Marriages.* Washington, D.C., American Psychiatric Press, Inc., 1988.

Gaylin, Willard. *Caring.* New York: Alfred A. Knopf, Inc., 1976.

Gibran, Kahlil. *The Prophet.* New York: Alfred A. Knopf, 1923.

Helmering, Doris Wild. *Happily Ever After: A Therapist's Guide to Taking the Fight out and Putting the Fun Back into Your Marriage.* New York: Warner Books, Inc., 1986.

Hendricks, Gay and Kathlyn Hendricks. *Conscious Loving: the Journey to Co-Commitment: A Way to Be Fully Together without Giving up Yourself.* New York: Bantam Books, 1990.

Hendrix, Harville. *Getting the Love You Want: A Guide for Couples.* New York: Henry Holt and Company, Inc., 1988.

Horner, Althea. *Being and Loving,* Revised Edition. Northvale, New Jersey: Jason Aronson Inc., 1990.

Jeffers, Susan. *Opening Our Hearts to Men: Transform Pain, Loneliness and Anger into Trust, Intimacy and Love.* New York: Fawcett Columbine, 1989.

Josselson, Ruthellen. *The Space Between Us: Exploring the Dimensions of Human Relationships.* San Francisco, Jossey-Bass, Inc., Publishers, 1992.

Kinder, Melvyn and Connell Cowan. *Husbands and Wives: Exploding the Marital Myths/Deepening Love and Desire*. New York: Clarkson N. Potter, Inc., Publishers, 1989.

Klagsbrun, Francine. *Married People: Staying Together in the Age of Divorce*. New York: Bantam Books, 1985.

Lerner, Harriett. *The Dance of Anger: A Woman's Guide to Changing the Patterns of Intimate Relationships*. New York: Harper & Row Publishers, 1985.

_____. *The Dance of Intimacy*. New York: Harper & Row, Publishers, Inc., 1989.

Medved, Diane. *The Case Against Divorce*. New York: Donald I. Fine, Inc., 1989.

Mellan, Olivia. *Money Harmony: Resolving Money Conflicts in Your Life and Relationships*. New York: Walker and Company, 1994.

Miller, Alice. *Banished Knowledge: Facing Childhood Injuries*. New York: Doubleday, 1990.

_____. *Breaking Down the Wall of Silence: The Liberating Experience of Facing Painful Truth*. New York: Dutton, 1991.

_____. *For Your Own Good: Hidden Cruelty in Childrearing and the Roots of Violence*. New York: FSG, 1983.

_____. *Paths of Life: Seven Scenarios*. New York: Pantheon Books, 1998.

_____. *Prisoners of Childhood: The Drama of the Gifted Child and the Search for the True Self*. New York: Basic Books, 1981.

_____. *Thou Shalt Not Be Aware: Society's Betrayal of the Child.* New York: FSG, 1984.

_____. *The Truth Will Set You Free: Overcoming Emotional Blindness and Finding Your True Adult Self.* Basic Books, 2001.

_____. *The Untouched Key: Tracing Childhood Trauma in Creativity and Destructiveness.* New York: Doubleday, 1990.

Minirth, Frank and Mary Alice Minirth, Brian and Deborah Newman and Robert and Susan Hemfelt. *Passages of Marriage: Five Growth Stages That Will Take Your Marriage to Greater Intimacy and Fulfillment.* Nashville: Thomas Nelson Publishers, 1991.

Myers, Michael F., *Doctors' Marriages: A Look at the Problems and Their Solutions*, Second Edition. New York, Plenum Medical Book Company, 1994, 1998.

Notarius, Clifford and Howard Markman. *We Can Work It Out: Making Sense Out of Marital Conflict.* New York: G.P. Putnam's Sons, 1993.

Parrott, Les and Leslie. *Meditations on Proverbs for Couples.* Grand Rapids, Michigan: Zondervan Publishing House, A division of Harper Collins Publishers, 1997.

Paul, Jordan and Margaret Paul. *Do I Have to Give Up Me to Be Loved By You?* Minneapolis: CompCare Publishers, 1983.

Paul, Jordan. *From Conflict to Caring.* Minneapolis, Minn.: CompCare Publishers, 1989.

_____. *If You Really Loved Me: For Everyone Who is a Parent and Everyone Who Has Been a Child.* Minneapolis: CompCare Publishers, 1987.

Payson, Eleanor D. *The Wizard of OZ and other Narcissists: Coping with the One-Way Relationship in Work, Love and Family.* Royal Oak, MI: Julian Day Publications, 2002.

Pines, Ayala Malach. *Keeping the Spark Alive, Preventing Burnout in Love and Marriage.* New York: St. Martin's Press. 1987.

Pittman, Frank. *Private Lies: Infidelity and the Betrayal of Intimacy.* New York: W. W. Norton & Co., Inc., 1989.

Prather, Hugh and Gayle. *I Will Never Leave You: How Couples Can Achieve the Power of Lasting Love.* New York: Bantam Books, 1995.

Rubin, Theodore Isaac. *Real Love: What It Is and How to Find It.* New York: Continuum Publishing Co., 1990.

Scarf, Maggie. *Intimate Partners: Patterns in Love and Marriage.* New York: Random House, Inc., 1987.

Simmons, Drew Phillip. *A Path of Peace with God, A Journey of Affirmations.* Venice, California: Fire of Faith Publications, 2003.

Sinetar, Marsha. *Living Happily Ever After.* New York: Villard Books, 1990.

Smedes, Lewis B. *Caring & Commitment: Learning to Live the Love We Promise.* New York: Harper & Row, Publishers, Inc., 1989.

_____. *Forgive & Forget: Healing the Hurts We Don't Deserve.* New York: Harper & Row, Publishers, Inc., 1984.

Stettbacher, J. Konrad. *Making Sense of Suffering: The Healing Confrontation with Your Own Past.* New York: Dutton, 1991.

Stone, Hal and Sidra L. Stone. *Partnering: A New Kind of Relationship*. Novato, CA: New World Library, 2000.

Tanenbaum, Joe. *Male and Female Relationships*. Costa Mesa, CA: Robert Erdmann Publishing Co. 1990.

Weiss, Robert S. *Staying the Course: The Emotional and Social Lives of Men Who Do Well at Work*. New York: The Free Press, 1990.

Welwood, John. *Journey of the Heart: The Path of Conscious Love*. New York: Harper-Collins Publishers, 1990.

Whitfield, Charles L. *Boundaries and Relationships: Knowing, Protecting and Enjoying the Self*. Deerfield Beach, FL: Health Communications, Inc., 1993.

Wile, Daniel B. *After the Honeymoon, How Conflict Can Improve Your Relationship*. New York: John Wiley & Sons, Publishers, Inc., 1988.

Woititz, Janet Geringer. *Struggle for Intimacy*. Deerfield, Florida: Health Communications, Inc., 1990.

Womack, William and Fred F. Stauss. *The Marriage Bed: Renewing, Love, Friendship, Trust and Romance*. Oakland, California: New Harbinger Publications, Inc., 1986.